SETTING UP HOME

SETTING UP HOME

Little, Brown and Company Boston·Toronto

Original room designs by Mary Gilliatt
and photographed by Bruce Hemming

Library of Congress Catalog Card No. 85-824-06

First American Edition

Original room designs by Mary Gilliatt
and photography by Bruce Hemming

Published simultaneously in Canada
by Little, Brown & Company (Canada) Limited

Printed in Italy

Little, Brown and Company
Boston · Toronto

CONTENTS

Exciting prospect though it is, setting up your first home can be fairly daunting financially. Whether you're embarking on it as a couple or on your own, it's going to bring you face to face with the realities of serious money planning, probably for the first time in your life. Having said that, it's fatal to take the gloomy view that budgeting is all about what you can't have. Quite the contrary – it's simply wise buying that is backed up by sensible, careful planning in advance.

If a budget imposes limits that's all to the good because setting up home is an expensive business and mistakes are correspondingly expensive and difficult to undo. You're more likely to end up with the home of your dreams if you proceed with caution, deciding what you can afford and when, which are the essential items and how to pay or save for them, and how to make what money you have at your disposal stretch in order to meet your needs and tastes.

Designing and decorating your own home is an exciting and rewarding challenge; so many elements have to be considered, from color and texture to the positioning of the furniture, until you achieve the look you like. It takes time and patience though. A comfortable but sophisticated room such as this is not created overnight.

Because your home has a great deal to do with your happiness and comfort this sort of budgeting calls as much for imagination and ingenuity as for efficient money management. After all, what you want is as important as what you can afford; you just have to be that much cleverer about achieving it. Even if your bank balance puts a brake on your spending the sky's the limit as far as bright ideas are concerned. Look for realistic ways of achieving the sort of 'feel' you want in your home.

While a joint budget gives you more scope and more money to play with, it also means more compromises to be made as you try to satisfy two sets of very personal tastes and priorities; setting up on your own in a studio or small apartment at least means you have only yourself to please.

Creating a pleasant, comfortable place to live in can be complicated, costly, time-consuming and often frustrating. All the more reason for proper and thorough planning; then, if there are pitfalls you're prepared for them, if not you'll be agreeably surprised. Remember there's no problem without a solution; getting there might be a headache but the chances are that you'll come up with something original, different and exactly right for your purposes.

So the aim of this book is twofold: to give you a clear picture of what setting up home entails without making light of the possible difficulties, and also to provide plenty of ideas, options and sound advice to make up for lack of cash. Decorating and designing the interior, organizing available space, treating and furnishing individual rooms, renovating and repairing furniture, improvising brilliantly with what you've got ... you'll find help and inspiration on all these subjects but with one big difference – a sharp eye to what it costs and to making the most of everything for as little as possible. What you need, how to choose it and how to get it more cheaply, indulging your ideas without going in over your head – that's what this book is all about.

Use it a a blueprint for planning your home from start to finish or pick and choose among its many possibilities to solve a particular problem. Whether you're converting a whole house or rearranging a studio, it will help you cope practically and sensibly. Setting up home is an important step and a costly one but don't forget it's also a very exciting one.

Here's how to enjoy it – and afford it.

/// Where will you live and in what sort of home? Should you rent, or can you afford to buy? Most likely, two factors will immediately influence your answers: where you work and how much you can afford to pay. Only when you have determined your limits – financial and geographical – can you set out to find the house, apartment or condominium that suits you best.

TO RENT OR BUY?

The soaring cost of real estate in the United States has forced many a potential home buyer into the rental market instead, and unfortunately, the truth is that most people operating on a tight budget are not in a position to buy a home. With the average price of a house in America hovering around $100,000, it generally takes two incomes and a hefty down payment for a first-time buyer mortgage.

If circumstances currently are making a home of your own impossible, don't despair. Renting a home may not be as desirable in the long run, but the (generally) lower rent payments you can expect may enable you to set aside enough cash to eventually make a down payment on a property of your own. And in the meantime, you can have fun fixing up your rented home to your satisfaction.

RENTING A HOUSE OR APARTMENT

Looking for a house or apartment to rent can be one of life's most frustrating activities, but with the right approach, it not only will prove to be fun, but you will end up with a home that meets your needs. Before you begin to look, make a list of your requirements: distance from work, number of bedrooms, price, furnished vs. unfurnished, etc. Then look through the classified ads in the local paper for the area where you'd like to live and determine what is available in your price range. Even if you ultimately find your home through some other means, the classifieds are probably the best place to start. In areas of the country where there is fierce competition for housing, as in New York and Southern California, you will have to cultivate many sources of leads. Word-of-mouth is an effective one – let people know that you're looking. Also case the neighborhoods that interest you and look for "For Rent" signs. Rental agencies, while not always what they're cracked up to be, have worked for some apartment hunters.

If you're limited by funds or opportunity, 'keep it simple' is a good rule. A neutral carpet and spanking white paint make a good background for treasured possessions. The carefully positioned greenery provides life and color, linking with the green of the leafy tree outside.

When looking at a potential rental, there are a number of questions you should ask. Is the building quiet? (You can determine this for yourself by listening for noise filtering through the walls and ceiling.) Does the building seem well maintained? Are the other buildings in the neighborhood well kept up? (Again, you'll be the best judge.) Is there parking? Is the building well lit at night? Is there any sort of security system, such as a doorman or an electric gate? What shape is the plumbing in? (Turn on the taps to determine.) Who pays utilities? Are pets and/or children allowed? Does any kitchen equipment come with the house or apartment? Does the layout suit your lifestyle? What sort of lease is available? What deposits or fees are required?

If the house or apartment needs some work

Plain painted walls and a stripped and varnished floor focus attention on well-styled furniture (right), with a variety of lighting effects to change the mood as required. The warmth of stained wood flooring looks equally good with lots of stripped wood and rattan (below).

before it will satisfy you, try to determine the landlord's position on these matters. Will you be allowed to paint? Can the orange carpet tiles in the bathroom be torn up? Is the exuberant floral wallpaper in the kitchen expendible? Will the landlord install a shower in the existing tub-only bathroom?

Try also to think of the apartment or house in terms of a year-round residence. Is it apt to be sweltering in the summer and un-air-conditioned? Who controls the heat in the winter, the tenant or the landlord?

It's difficult to weigh all these factors and make an informed, intelligent decision about renting an apartment or house when there hordes of potential tenants competing with you in a sellers' market. But having as many facts as possible at the outset will help you find – and rent – the most comfortable home for your requirements.

BUYING A HOME

If you've been squirreling away money for a while or have suddenly had a windfall and can now afford to make a down payment on a home of your own, congratulations. And start looking for a home right away. The economic advantages are so great, it doesn't pay you to rent a day longer than you have to.

Home ownership is not without its pitfalls, however, and here it is doubly important to assess your needs before signing on the dotted line; if you decide you can't stand the home once you've bought it, you'll be stuck until you can find another buyer.

Basically in choosing property to buy, you'll have to decide between a condominium or coop and a house, and between an old property or a newer one. Again, your finances will largely dictate what you end up with. Condominiums and coop apartments tend to be less expensive than single-family houses, although there are exceptions in both categories. The same holds true with old homes and newer ones: generally, you get more for your money with an older home, but you'll often also have higher repair bills. There are, however, inexpensive new homes and costly older ones that disprove the rule.

BUYING NEW

With new property you have the assurance of knowing that what you see is more or less what you get. The roof, plumbing, heating, insulation and wiring should all be of good quality and in good order: no nasty surprises such as hidden leaks and faults. But this isn't always the case, and because there are some developers less conscientious than others, it is important to have even the newest of buildings inspected properly. The structure should be sound, the walls and woodwork newly painted, and such things as light switches, wall sockets (not usually enough) door knobs, locks and taps provided. There will be bathroom and kitchen basics and possibly a stove and if not a dishwasher and washing machine, refrigerator, with some carpet and other basics thrown in. What you usually sacrifice are spacious period rooms, detail and character, a mature garden and, finally, the sort of atmosphere that only years of loving care create. What you gain, apart from the peace of mind that comes from knowing the property is sound, are purchasing incentives from the developer.

BUYING OLD

An older property can be ultimately very rewarding, particularly if you buy cheaply because the building is in a bad state of repair and you are prepared, even eager, to put a great deal of hard and patient work as

well as more money into its restoration. If the time and the area are both right, when you come to sell, you could make a considerable profit. New houses do not increase in value as quickly as older ones.

If the house is surprisingly inexpensive then it may be very run-down, possibly even semi-derelict, which means you will have to restore everything from the roof to floor joists as well as undertaking such major and expensive tasks as dry rot treatment, installing or updating central heating, rewiring, re-plumbing, re-flooring, and kitchen and bathroom remodeling. In addition, there are minor improvements such as new light switches and sockets, lighting fixtures, door knobs and the renovation of walls, woodwork and paintwork, all of which can add up to a frightening amount of money.

This old bathroom was totally revamped. The toilet and tank were relocated and replaced with a storage cabinet next to an old-fashioned tub surrounded by traditional white tiles. The walls were painted a very pale blue and the dormer window edged in a striking print border.

Some of the major modernization and improvement jobs, such as roofing or bringing the structure up to the current building code, might qualify for subsidized low-interest home improvement loans. Check with your local city or county government for information. Some states also offer tax deductions for improvements that conserve energy, such as insulation and solar heating.

Much of the decorating and improving you can do yourself for the cost of the materials. Never attempt work such as plumbing or wiring unless you know what you are doing; it is more sensible to pay for an expert than to make costly and possibly dangerous mistakes.

Older properties do need more care and concern and often a great deal of money spent on them and this can seem daunting at first, particularly if a place has been allowed to fall into a bad state of disrepair. On the plus side, the end result is well worth it, both in terms of satisfaction and investment value.

FROM HOME TO ASSET

Having gotten your priorities clear in your mind, you should always look at a property with an eye to re-selling. At this stage you may well think you will stay for life but, in practice, most first-time buyers move on within a few years. So you should look for something that is not too idiosyncratic or in an undesirable location or badly designed. It is worth remembering that one-bedroom properties do not re-sell very quickly.

Looking for the potential in a new building is mostly a question of finding what appeals and will suit your lifestyle and pocket. Many are specially designed these days for young couples or single people buying a first home.

Looking for the potential in an older property in bad condition means using both your imagination and good sense to see whether you can make an attractive, comfortable, practical home and, with luck, even a fat profit, out of something most other people have rejected. The rooms may be in a bad state, but are they basically well-proportioned? In spite of the doubtful superficial appearance of the building, is it basically sound or will it need expensive structural repairs? Could windows be altered to let in more light? Or partition walls be pulled down or put up to make better use of the existing space? If the bathroom is inadequate how could it be improved? Could the kitchen space be improved by extending or simply reorganizing? Are the floorboards sound underneath the surface dirt and coverings? Is the house immediately habitable?

If you do happen on a house that you feel might possess such assets under the grime of time, try to view it on your own and explore it at leisure. This is usually impossible with houses that are still inhabited, but you might be allowed to do it with a more run-down property.

The fireplace creates a natural focal point even when not in use. These two (above) show how rough brick and a concealed spotlight make an effective showcase. And how neat a frame surrounding a hearth can look in a modern setting.

Never rip out in haste what you could turn to your advantage. An old fireplace and wooden shutters (left) were rejuvenated by a good sanding and a fresh coat of paint: hard work but not expensive in terms of materials. Traditional accessories provide the final touch.

FIREPLACES

There are as many types of fireplaces as there are styles of rooms, and if you are considering replacing yours, you will find a vast selection to choose from, either secondhand originals rescued from buildings wrecked by demolition companies or faithful reproductions in brick, stone, marble, wood or cast iron.

However, personal taste alone should not dictate your final choice; remember the age and style of the room where you are going to install it, and, even more important, its proportions. Nothing looks more out of place than a too-small fireplace in a large room, or a too-large one beneath a low ceiling. If you want to use the fireplace you will have to check the suitability of the flue size too, or you may find the fire will not draw properly when you go to light it; an architect or fireplace dealer should be able to advise you on this sort of thing.

Once you have settled on the exact style of fireplace you want, consider all the extras: hearth, slips, firebacks and screens. Again there is a vast selection of styles and materials and it is a good idea, if you can, to consider several of them with your intended fireplace before you decide which looks best (a high-standing, ornate fire screen in a large fireplace, for example).

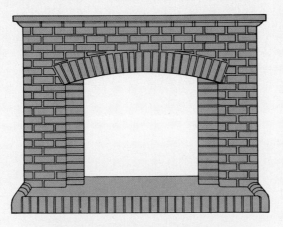

A conventional brick surround

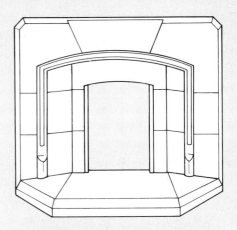

Plain, usually local, stone

Elegant sculptured marble

Traditional waxed oak

Victorian cast iron

Ornate tiled side slips

The success of this room rests on clever use of attractive but inexpensive materials, combined with economic use of more costly fabrics and items. A sophisticated gray/rust design fabric has been used to frame the window, with an inexpensive white paper blind to screen the actual window area. Small amounts of matching and coordinating fabrics have been used to make cushion covers and fabric panels.

The warm terracotta color of the fabric is echoed in the use of natural textures such as the inexpensive but hardwearing sisal flooring used throughout, and a selection of baskets and terracotta plant pots; the fireplace is made of marble and warm, waxed pine. Furniture is a mixture of improvisation and high style; an economical homemade window seat and occasional table help balance the budget and make this room very smart and a little special

Elegant and inexpensive fabric has been draped over a gray-painted pole to create a pair of instant dress curtains for minimum effort and expense. A simple white paper blind is sufficient to screen the window area without detracting from the effect.

If you can't afford to buy much of a fabric you like, use it sparingly but effectively. In this room, two coordinating designs have been made into cushion covers, the remnants stretched over padded plywood and fastened to the walls as a decoration (reflected in the mirrors). Pieces of fabric could be framed and displayed in the same way or used to cover door panels.

The occasional table was quickly and simply made using a circular terracotta plant pot topped with circle of glass. The pot is filled with sand for stability and matches those used for plants elsewhere in the room.

Look for new ways to use familiar objects. Here cane baskets not only provide useful storage, but also make good table tops for drinks and magazines. A grass fan makes an unusual but effective table mat.

Note how the fine marble hearth becomes the perfect place to display baskets of green plants in summer – far more attractive than a gaping chimney.

despite their cost-cutting tactics – a case of using your money where it has the greatest effect.

But elegant chairs and tables haven't simply been chosen for their good looks. Bauhaus design chairs have been adapted in clear Lucite to make them almost invisible, an important consideration in a room which doubles as sitting and dining room, particularly since the chairs are stylish and comfortable enough to use as both easy and dining chairs.

The square-cut table with its smoked glass and brass trim is stylish enough to look good when not used for eating and blends into rather than stands out of the decorative scheme. Storage, too, is unobtrusive yet on display: glass shelves in the alcoves, natural wicker baskets and the fabric-covered window seat with hinged lid. The finished effect is to have a warm, inviting room that is also up-to-the-minute and sophisticated.

Improvised seating doubles as storage in a room short of space but not ideas. Plywood box structure with foam cushion lid has been covered in a creamy white wool fabric. The lid lifts up to reveal lift-out wire storage baskets like those found in dishwashers, ideal for dishes.

If you are short of both space and possessions, resort to mirrors. Here pre-drilled mirror sections fitting exactly between a series of glass shelves are a lot easier to handle and less expensive than a sheet of mirror to fit the space, and just as effective. The room seems twice the size, lighter and brighter with the reflection of lights and window.

An architect's office exploits the fine details of this old warehouse: lovely arched windows and double doors are left unadorned, while stripped and polished floorboards emphasize a generous floor area. Functional metal shelving makes ideal, instantly available storage with brightly striped deck chairs providing cheap but comfortable seating. Plenty of plants on makeshift pedestals or hung from the ceiling help to avoid any suggestion of a barnlike atmosphere in this large space.

There are certain obvious pitfalls that can be fairly easily avoided. The area itself, for instance. Careful scrutiny of potential neighbors and other streets in the vicinity will tell you whether it is an up-and-coming district or one that is on its way down. If your immediate neighbors treat their garden like a junk heap and spoil the look of the place that's a good enough reason for not taking the house; there's no guarantee they'll leave or mend their ways and, as time goes by with no sign of improvement, the general unsightliness could become a source of nagging annoyance to you.

What about other houses nearby? Perhaps many of them still look scruffy, but are there signs that several are being renovated? Or is there an air of universal neglect?

Try to view the property during a normal working day as well as weekends or after office hours. Stroll around to see what the area is like during the week. Is there a particular source of noise or dirt? What about traffic or a popular bar that might be a source of nuisance at night and on weekends? Are there sufficient parking facilities?

If you are looking at a coop or condominium, find out about maintenance charges or any hidden bills.

Many people choose a condo or coop rather than a house for reasons of security and because they do not want to be bothered with all the things that could go wrong in a house. What they often forget is that you have to pay for these privileges and that, for good reasons, there is generally no guarantee that maintenance charges will be kept at the same level from year to year.

PLANNING FOR THE FUTURE

If you plan to have a family, you should look for a home with at least two bedrooms. If you think you might need to offer a home to elderly parents sometime in the future, you should make sure that there is a room they could call their own or space for adding on – perhaps a separate apartment, with cooking facilities, would be ideal for them and you.

Are there good schools nearby? What is the local public transportation system like? And the local shops? Will you be able to get to work easily? If the house is in a town or suburb, is there adequate play space within easy walking distance for children and pets? If it's an old house or apartment does it lend itself to modernization and improvement and, if so, can you tackle it or afford it? Too many people bite

To get your priorities straight before you make an offer for any property you should ask yourself these questions:

1 How many rooms do you need? Maximum number and minimum number.
2 What are you going to use them for?
3 Are the sizes of the rooms right for you and your family's needs?
4 How much space could be made multi-functional, e.g. could a dining room double as a playroom or study? Could the hall be used for dining?
5 Can the sort and number of rooms you need be provided from the existing space by either knocking down walls or making partitions or changing levels?
6 Is there attic or basement or roof space?
7 Is there room for an extension?
8 Will the garden need work? Could it be paved or made labor-saving?
9 Is the house sound? If not, how much work will it need and are you up to it physically, and can you afford it? If it's in need of extensive work, will there be sufficient funds on top of mortgage payments, taxes, utilities and other bills, for the home improvement loan that you'll almost certainly need? Bear in mind all the other new expenses like kitchen appliances, carpets, as well as do-it-yourself and renovation costs.
10 What is the parking/garage situation? Is there space for bicycles?
11 Is the house safe or can it be made safe for the very young or elderly?
12 Can you get your furniture in? If you own a large family heirloom or grand piano is there space for it?

Find out from the seller or knowledgeable third party:

1 What the nearest schools are like.
2 What both shopping facilities and public transportation are like.
3 If there are difficult or troublesome neighbors.
4 If there are any new roads, extensions to highways, housing developments, factories or educational establishments planned? It could mean an enormous increase in traffic and noise.
5 Whether there are any particular snags to the house. This can be difficult to find out but you should try.
6 How much the taxes and utility rates are.

Learn to show off your best features; these lovely stained glass door panels are framed with stripped pine and tiny terracotta tiles and provide a harmonious, warm background to the delicate flowers.

off more than they can chew in their initial enthusiasm and live to regret it. If there's a garden, what sort of state is it in and are there any potential hazards for children such as a pond or steps? Are there any new roads, extensions to highways or large developments like factories or supermarkets planned to be built nearby in the next few years? If the building is near a river or stream, is there any real risk of possible damage from flooding to be considered?

However much you like a place on first sight, and particularly if you fall for the cherry tree in the garden or for the beautiful kitchen, don't buy on the strength of these alone. Try to talk yourself out of it, not into it. Ask yourself all the most awkward questions you can think of before making up your mind. It is easier to be tough and efficient before you convince yourself you want the place or have struck up a good relationship with the seller. There is a lot of money at stake and also your health, happiness and peace of mind to be considered. A wrong decision could ruin your life and involve you in great financial hardship. Think long and hard – and realistically - before you make up your mind about committing yourself to a particular property.

An unusually shaped window tends to be best left to speak for itself. This elegant five-paned arch needs no fussy blinds or curtains which would only confuse its fine shape. Instead, miniblinds provide neat but effective screening.

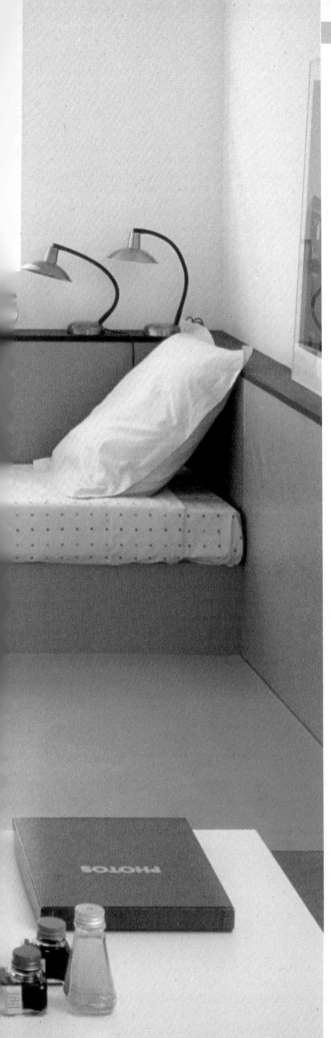

/// Where you begin your makeover plan will depend on many factors: whether you're renting or buying; what improvements are most urgent, and how much you can afford.

If you're renting your home, any structural defects happily are the province of the landlord. And with any luck, your landlord is the type who attends to repairs promptly. It's best not to begin decorating until the repairs are completed. There's nothing like hanging wallpaper in the kitchen or bathroom and then have a plumber knock a hole through it to fix a leaky pipe. Also make sure that your landlord agrees to let you carry out your decorative scheme. One person's improvement is another's disaster. And depending on the terms of your lease or rental agreement, you might find yourself liable for the cost of undoing your handiwork after you move out.

One of the benefits of home ownership, of course, is the fact that you can make any changes you choose to your property, and only your bank account and local building code can overrule you. The exception, of course, comes with condos and coop apartments. Often, the governing homeowners' association may have the right to veto your plans if they affect the structure of the building.

If you're renovating a single-family house, the responsibility for repairs rests solely on your shoulders (and in your pocketbook), but you have the freedom to do virtually anything you please, as long as it conforms to the local building code. Before buying your house, you should have the property inspected by a professional building inspector to assess its condition and to detect any hidden faults. (Such an inspection is an excellent idea because it eliminates most unpleasant surprises about your house.) If the inspection turns up any urgent problems, attend to those before attempting any cosmetic or decorative improvements. If there are several things that need attention, don't feel over-whelmed; often you can handle the repairs in stages.

THE STAGED PLAN

It's too much to hope that you can afford to have everything done in one almighty blitz. So you need a stage-by-stage plan of action, dictated by your bank balance. Attend first to any structural repairs and alterations: rot, termite damage, plasterwork that

Clean, simple lines of built-in furniture and cool neutral colors are given warmth and impact with clever use of primary color: a warm yellow floor and touches of dramatic red. A narrow shelf around the room at waist level not only makes a natural break, but also provides useful storage.

needs to be fixed, floor repairs, rewiring, re-plumbing, heating. When you're quite sure that the structure is in good repair, then you can tackle the decoration. Go on to the equipping and decorating of the most necessary rooms in the house like kitchen and bathroom, followed by other rooms in due course.

If you aren't working with an inspector's report and decide to take a chance on the structure, there's quite a lot you can do yourself to make a sensible appraisal of the house both inside and out. But do bear in mind nothing can take the place of a proper inspector's report. You can have one done covering just the essentials, or a more detailed and correspondingly more expensive one done, depending on your needs and finances. An inspector has a trained eye and can spot things you might overlook.

Rent an extension ladder and take a look at the roof. Are there shingles missing or any obviously worn patches? Does the chimney lean over? Examine walls thoroughly; look for uneven masonry and bulges – both signs of movement. What condition are the clapboards in? Does brickwork need repointing – i.e., is the mortar between the bricks in a bad state? If so, this can cause dampness and should be dealt with. Make a note of any cracks; the usual problem areas are under window ledges, around damaged downpipes and on exposed chimneys. Are the gutters broken, sagging or blocked? Are they draining properly? Are gutters and down-pipes firmly attached?

TERMITES

Termites are more of a problem in some parts of the country than in others, but in nearly every state, termite inspection is advisable if not mandatory before a house is sold.

Although much is made of the threat termites pose to a structure, the fact is that it takes many years for them to do much serious damage. The most destructive variety are subterranean termites, which live in the soil. Although termites can't tolerate exposure to sunlight or fresh air, they can gain access to the wood in your house if the structure is built on a slab, because the wooden members are at ground level. And even if your house is built on a masonry foundation, they can tunnel up to the wood if there is soil piled up around the foundation. A good rule of thumb to bear in mind is to keep wood 12 inches above the earth on the outside of the house and 30 inches above the ground on the inside. It's also a good idea to keep steps and porches clear of the ground by means of a stone or concrete platform. Metal termite shields on top of basement walls will also help keep termites at bay.

More damaging than termites, however, is common wood rot, which is caused by a fungus. It is wood rot that most frequently necessitates replacement of timbering in older homes.

PLACEMENT OF LIGHTS

Lighting needs careful planning at the early stages if you are to get the most out of your furnishing ideas. Recessed downlights make an excellent basic framework for general lighting, especially if equipped with a dimmer control. Add outlets near the floor for uplights to bounce light off the ceiling and to highlight plants; a dining area will need low, soft but direct light, or a rise and fall attachment which allows you to raise or lower a pendant light according to your mood. These are particularly effective used in dual-purpose rooms where you may only have a dining area which need lighting separately from the rest of the room. Spotlights give good directional light for working or reading and can be wall-, ceiling-, or table-mounted.

Dimmed recessed lights are perfect for creating a romantic, relaxed atmosphere and will barely be noticeable during the day. Some models are designed with a swivel action so that they can wash walls with light.

Low lighting centrally placed over the table on a long cord is useful for dining and is often adjustable for creating a change of atmosphere. It is essential to make sure that the lights will not dazzle diners.

INSIDE PLANNING

Examine the wiring. Are the switches and outlets reasonably modern? Does any wire you see look old or worn? If it looks old it is sensible to have it rewired. Get in a professional electrician and do not, unless you are properly qualified to do so, attempt to rewire it yourself.

While you are examining the wiring you should be thinking carefully about new outlets and also about lighting. Good lighting can transform your home but it needs to be well planned. Before you can even think about the number and position of sockets and

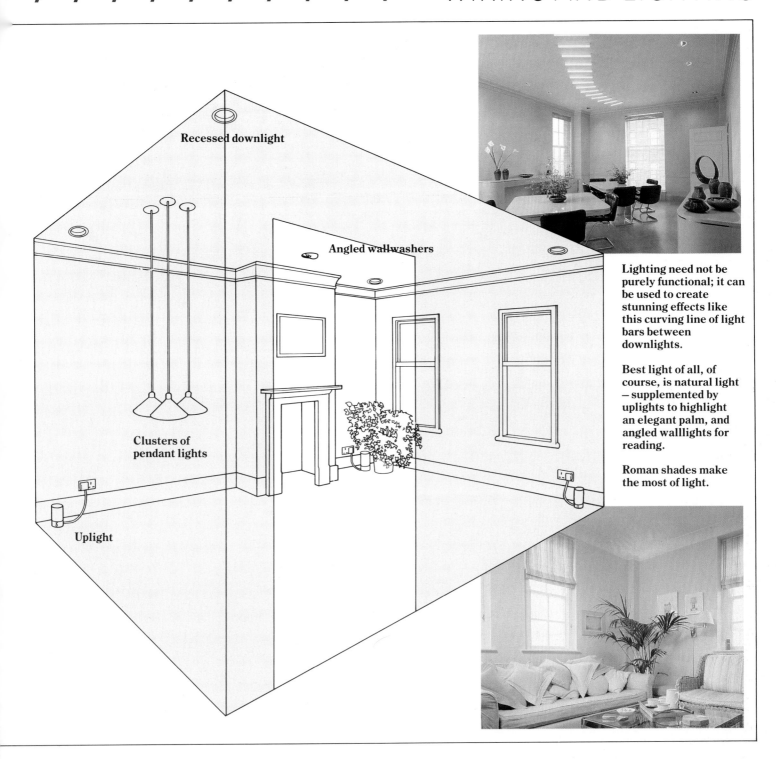

Recessed downlight

Angled wallwashers

Clusters of pendant lights

Uplight

Lighting need not be purely functional; it can be used to create stunning effects like this curving line of light bars between downlights.

Best light of all, of course, is natural light – supplemented by uplights to highlight an elegant palm, and angled walllights for reading.

Roman shades make the most of light.

switches you need to work out just how you want each room to be lit and what effect you are trying to achieve. Lighting can alter the shape and mood of a room; it can be functional or decorative or both.

If you are thinking of lowering ceilings for any reason – maybe to alter the proportions of a room or to help with heating cost – this is a good opportunity for installing recessed spots, downlights and wall-washers.

Putting in dimmer switches and special lighting effects to highlight furniture or paintings or objects in a room is best done at an early stage too; it can be

difficult and expensive to achieve if you wait until the room is decorated and furnished. Think of lighting as part of the framework like walls, floors and ceilings rather than as an afterthought. Work out in as much detail as possible a lighting scheme for each room in the house. How many different types of lights, how many sockets and switches and where they are to go. Get an estimate – or preferably several – for all the electrical work so that you can prepare a realistic budget for all this early essential work. Ask people who live in the area for the names of reliable electricians who have done satisfactory work.

One sure way of wasting money is to overlook some vital detail that has to be added later, long after the original job is done and at considerable expense. To avoid this, there is no substitute for a carefully thought out – and written out – check list. It should have two main headings: Services and Structure, subheaded as below and with space allowed for comments. Don't carry anything in your head: commit all your thoughts and ideas to paper. It would also be a sensible idea to devise some sort of system within the list itself. If you color code the items, for instance according to how urgent or necessary they are, you have only to glance at your list to see immediately how the whole plan is taking shape. Everyone's priorities will be different, but a basic list might be as follows:

SERVICES	STRUCTURE
Electricity	Roof
Gas	External walls
Heating	Internal walls
Ventilation	Floors
Water	Leaks
Plumbing	Insulation
Drainage	Cracks

BE REALISTIC

This is what you should have down on paper: a clear idea of what you can afford to spend, now and over the next few years (to be on the safe side, don't spend every last penny – keep a small amount aside for emergencies); a list of jobs in order of priority; a list of essential equipment.

Working all this out will have forced you to do a lot of hard thinking, to prune and discard what is unworkable, impractical and too expensive, and you will have a much firmer picture of your own tastes.

THE PRIORITIES

You must get the main structural work out of the way or at least taken care of financially before you move on to decoration and furnishings. But even if the major jobs are going to eat up all the spare money you have for some time to come, it doesn't hurt to allow for the final decorating stage in the master plan. It keeps the end in sight and gives you some idea of what you still have to spend.

Tackle the rooms in order of priority. Usually it reads like this: kitchen, bathroom, main bedroom, living room, followed by other rooms according to their needs. Decide on decoration schemes and work out the cost before thinking about furnishings. Even if you change your mind it's better to have a good plan to stray from than none at all. In fact, you're less likely to deviate from your list if you realize that it will increase your costs. However, you do have to allow for some flexibility just in case things don't go exactly as planned.

WHEN TO SAVE AND WHEN TO SPEND

There are some areas where you will just have to spend money and, again, it helps to list all essential tasks. Make one list for each room along the following lines:
Essential repairs/alterations
Electric wiring; checking and possible repair
Insulation
Lighting fixtures and their installation
Heating and attention to plumbing
Telephone installation where necessary
Painting or wall covering
Floor treatments: carpet, rugs, hardwood floors, painted finishes
Window treatments with appropriate hardware
Then make a room-by-room list of potential purchases. To keep spending in a realistic perspective, grade purchases as follows:

	LIVING AND DINING ROOM	KITCHEN AND UTILITY ROOM
NECESSITIES	Seating (comfortable and occasional)	Range (and its installation)
	Dining table and chairs	Sink(s) and drainboard(s)
	Bookshelves and storage	Storage – cabinets, shelves and their installation
	Coffee and side tables	Refrigerator/freezer
		Ventilation
		Vacuum cleaner, brushes brooms, dusters, cleaning equipment
		Pots and pans, dishes, cutlery, storage jars, cooking implements
		Ironing board and iron
USEFUL ADDITIONS	Serving table	Washing machine (with plumbing and installation)
	Cushions	Dryer
	Paintings, prints	Separate freezer
	Plants	Extractor hood for range
	Clocks, ornaments, collection of objects	Microwave oven
	Wastepaper baskets	Dishwasher
	Ashtrays, vases	Table linen, dish towels
		Extra china, glass, cutlery, serving dishes
		Laundry baskets
		Stepladder and basic tools
		Toaster, coffee maker and grinder, juice extractor, slow cooker, electric frypan
LUXURIES	Stereo equipment	Food processor
	Television and VCR	Rotisserie and separate grill
	Computer	Waste disposal unit

BATHROOM
Bathtub, basin, toilet
Tiling
Towel racks
Mirror
Towels, bathmat,
   washcloths
Hooks for clothes
Outlet for razor and
   hair dryer

BEDROOM
Beds, mattresses,
   pillows,
Sheets, comforters,
   blankets, pillowcases,
   bedspreads, dust ruffles
Storage
Dressing table
Nightstands
Chair

GARDEN
Lawn mower (if you
   have a lawn)
Garden tools
Plants
Clotheslines

Medicine cabinet
Stool or chair
Laundry basket
Plants, pictures

Bookshelves
Paintings, prints, plants
Headboards
Electric blankets
Rugs

Garden furniture
Sandbox for children
Planters
Barbecue equipment

Shower unit
Heated towel rail
Bidet
Carpet
Special make-up/shaving
   lights around mirror

Bedroom TV and stereo

Garden seat/swing
Pond or pool

QUICK, CLEVER FIX-UPS

While it's pointless to decorate until all the structural work is done, the thought of living in discomfort for months – or years, if the house is in a bad state – won't do much for morale. So there's a lot to be said for making one or two rooms reasonably comfortable without spending too much money. A coat of paint and some cheerful accessories will do the trick. Plants, prints, posters, a nice rug, a pretty shawl or tablecloth plus any decent furniture you may already have, as well as junk pieces spruced up with paint – these will all help to make a kitchen or living room tolerable.

Makeshift conditions in a bedroom can still give you some degree of comfort. A good mattress – even if you can't afford a proper bed yet – improvised storage such as shelves on bricks, curtained-off areas for hanging clothes, a chair, a rug and a well-positioned mirror will make life bearable. If you're down to one room, cover the bed/mattress with cushions to provide seating by day.

In fact, there's nothing to lose at this stage by experimenting, improvising, and adapting; anything to give you instant comfort and cheer. Desperation as well as necessity is often the mother of invention.

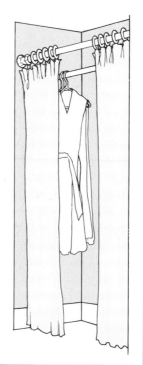

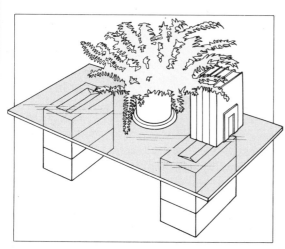

Curtains hung on a simple rod make an inexpensive, effective cover-up for clothes (top). Ordinary wicker chairs with back and arms set off in contrasting colors, simple prints and a profusion of plants bring this room alive (centre). Soft furnishings provide color accents. The improvised table (left) is simply a sheet of glass cut to a specified size and balanced on bricks.

CUTTING THE COSTS

The grand total, if you added it all up, would be horrendous but a sensibly staged plan will get you there in the end. Even so, there are various ways of pruning the expense without sacrificing comfort or the effect you're aiming at.

/ / / Shop around before you buy anything or before you have any work done. Get as much information as possible – from shops, magazines, consumer services, friends and neighbors. This applies just as much to employing contractors and decorators as to buying equipment – the inexpensive handyman can be a real find or a butcher who will cost you more in the long run. You might discover you have a real aptitude for do-it-yourself projects and are able to tackle many jobs. If you

This old chest took on a new life when it was painted black and trimmed with ochre to match the earthy colors of the stencilled pattern on the stripped floorboards. All surfaces were finally given a couple of coats of varnish to help them withstand routine wear and tear.

This room has combined a whole range of clever budget ideas to make the most of limited resources. A large pipe running the length of the room has been painted to blend with the ceiling and low improvised tables use bright red wood blocks and tops painted to imitate marble. A random selection of seating is visually united by a handsome oriental rug.

really are skilled, well and good; you'll enjoy doing it and save yourself a lot of money. If not, be wise and mature enough to admit your limitations and let a professional take over.

/ / / Don't despise secondhand. You can find excellent materials in good condition if you hunt around junkyards and demolition yards. Look for doors, fireplaces, banisters, moldings, flooring, old tiles, old bricks. Keep your eyes open for dumpsters outside houses in prosperous areas. If you're lucky you'll come across some good discards – bathtubs, basins, fireplaces; even finding a complete set of kitchen cabinets in reasonably good condition is not unknown. Patience and perseverance will be your best allies. And keep an open mind – you may find things you didn't

know you were looking for!

/ / / Look for discounts on electrical appliances or buy closeouts or scratched goods from reliable firms.

/ / / Buy linens, towels, china, glass and cutlery at sales or from discount shops.

/ / / Scan local newspaper columns, for interesting trades and sales of private goods as well as garage or tag sale, furniture sale and auction announcements.

/ / / Haunt the scruffier antique, junk and secondhand shops for furniture. Old chairs and tables, particularly old office equipment, can often be bought very cheaply. It can then be stripped, painted, lacquered or stained to suit your personal needs and preferences.

*F*ew of us can afford to have our very own gym or exercise room, however keen we are on keeping fit and working out. This room solves the problem perfectly. It isn't large but there is plenty of room for exercise – you would even be able to do energetic aerobics, which can take up a considerable space. The sofa is actually a futon on a wooden base which opens out, so at night you have a bed which is not only attractive, but also very comfortable and practical.

As befits a room with a serious purpose, decoration is minimal, almost spartan, but is bright and punchy enough to get the adrenalin going. Bright white is given added warmth and color with plenty of brilliant red and the natural glow of varnished wood. Lines are deliberately kept straight and simple: the floorboards have been left bare, blinds are used instead of curtains, and the furnishings are utilitarian – a tubular chair and simple wood-based futon – but brightly colored.

Stripped and varnished floor adds a natural warmth to the room and is perfect for floor exercises and equipment. It is essential that the boards be sanded perfectly smooth with no snags or sharp nails to catch on bare feet and limbs, then given several coats of clear polyurethane varnish to protect them.

Two recesses on either side of the chimney breast make natural closets, fitted here with mirrored doors to maximize space and provide head-to-toe reflections for avid exercisers.

Thin cane blind at the window is simple but functional, echoing the natural honey color of the varnished wood floor.

Bright red futon sofa bed provides somewhere to sit during the day and a double bed for nighttime. It unfolds quickly and easily onto a pine slatted base which is fastened by a simple rope and cleat device.

Red wall grid with special clips is perfect for space-saving vertical storage of sports equipment or clothes in frequent use.

Plain white walls and woodwork with a few bright primary prints focuses attention on the floor area and the room's main purpose.

During the day the room makes a perfect home gymnasium. There is plenty of empty floor area to stretch out an exercise mat or position a favorite piece of equipment and full-length mirrors for observing if progress is being made. A futon sofa and easy chair in bright red tubular metal and canvas strike just the right note: their lines are simple, yet both pieces of furniture provide the sort of surface that is perfect for collapsing onto and relaxing after some strenuous exercise.

At bedtime the futon swiftly unfolds into a comfortable double bed – simply throw over a comforter and a couple of pillows and it's ready. Long mirrors open to reveal a pair of double closets, cleverly using two niches behind the sofa. For those with a little money to spare and no need for such generous closet space, this area can be utilized in other ways; a shower unit installed behind one of those sets of mirrors would be an excellent and highly appropriate substitute.

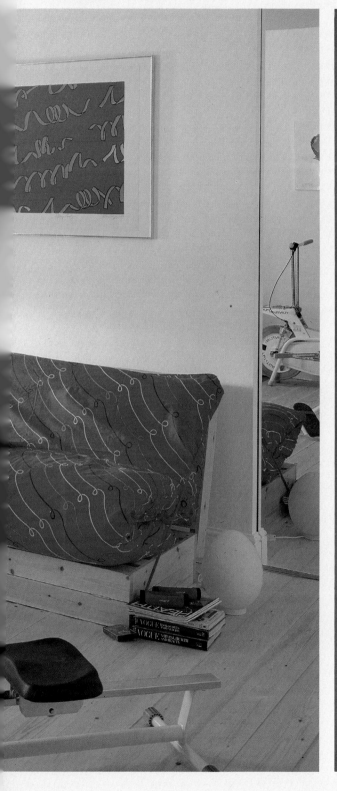

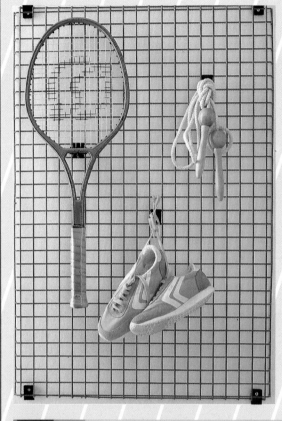

A simple, bright red wall grid makes ideal storage for sports equipment which often needs to be stored where air can circulate freely to prevent damage from mildew. Here racket, athletic shoes and jump rope look good on display.

At nighttime, the futon sofa bed unfolds to make a comfortable bed on a pine slatted base. It fits neatly between the mirrored closet doors; comforter, pillows and bed linen are neatly stored in the top of the closet. The futon is naturally low so there is no need for a nightstand, simply an egg-shaped floor light which is also a bedside lamp.

Ambitious extensions such as these above are usually best designed by a professional who will make the most imaginative and economical use of the space available. Always consider the final fittings and furniture in the preliminary planning to create the most pleasing effect.

GETTING STARTED

The amount of professional assistance you need will depend on how complicated the project you're undertaking is and on your skill level in the areas of interior design and construction. If you are inexperienced and your home needs a lot of structural work, it would probably be best to hire professionals to take care of the most important jobs. A general contractor, for example, will be familiar with the local building codes and will obtain permits for the work as part of his job.

Before calling in a professional, however, you should have some ideas about what you want in the remodeled rooms. It is very useful at this stage to put your ideas down on paper. Try drawing up a floor plan for each affected room. (See page 43 for guidelines.) Also make a complete list of what must be done in each room. Both the list and the floor plan will be useful points of reference when you first approach professionals. Once the final plans are

nailed down, there will be plenty of time to refine them before construction begins.

In all likelihood, a general contractor will be a necessary adviser if you are tackling major construction. The services contractors offer vary somewhat; some contractors have expanded businesses that offer design services as well as project management. All, however, coordinate the work of the subcontractors, and it is a delicate art – making certain that the electrician has completed the wiring for a garbage disposer before the plumber arrives to install it, for example, or that the base cabinets are complete with wooden trim before the tiling subcontractor arrives to lay the countertops. Although you can save considerable money by hiring the subcontractors and scheduling their work yourself, you can also find yourself embroiled in a nightmare if you're a novice. In the long run, it's usually best to hire a general contractor.

If you have the resources, an experienced interior

the finished work, including plumbing and electrical connections. If inspection seems like an annoyance, remember that its primary purpose is to protect you against incompetence.

PREPARING A SPECIFICATION

Even if you are not embarking on major structural work it is still important to put down on paper, in as much detail as you can manage, every single job that has to be tackled. Ideally, it should be so clear that whoever is doing the job has no need to ask for explanations in your absence. Even if you are doing all the work yourself, it is still helpful to write everything down and safer to tick items off against a checklist than to rely on memory. These items can include such things as:

/ / / Any work stipulated and recommended by your inspector.

/ / / Work that you can see needs doing; obvious and necessary repairs/alterations.

/ / / If you have a mortgage, any work the lender insists on as a condition of the loan (e.g. reinforcing the chimney).

/ / / Any work you must carry out in order to qualify for some sort of loan.

/ / / Work required by the public health department, or department of building safety.

/ / / Any additional work you want to have done.

When you are sure you have not left anything out, divide up the work into what needs doing on the exterior and what should be done inside. Do this room by room and floor by floor.

/ / / State how many coats of paint you want, specifying that all cracks be filled and old, flaky paint removed.

/ / / Name the makes of any appliances you want. Specify the exact dimensions, if possible; and say exactly where you want them installed.

/ / / Draw up a lighting and heating plan showing exactly where you want all outlets and radiators sited and specify where you want lights positioned.

/ / / If you are having something removed from a room say what is going to go in its place, just in case there should be some difficulty.

/ / / Finally you will need to draw up a decoration schedule for each room, but see chapter on walls, floors and windows, pages 53-73.

designer or space planner can help you plan your interior space to suit your needs and taste. A planner may also function as a buffer against the tribulations of a remodeling. If you hire a space planner in a purely consultive role, you might find his or her services less expensive than you had feared.

Each community has its own building code based on the realities of the area it governs. These codes apply to electrical, plumbing, and construction work, but not to simple redecorating. If you're not working with a contractor, call your local planning agency or building inspector for information about obtaining permits for the work you're having done. Be sure to find out how long it will take to obtain the permits. Plumbing and electrical subcontractors can usually obtain their own permits. Once you've applied for permits, you can expect a series of on-site visits from a building inspector, whose job it is to check the new foundation (if you're adding on); the rough work, such as framing, electrical, and plumbing; and

This conservatory style extension doubles as kitchen and spacious dining room with lots of glass, white paint and a decorative black and white tiled floor, which is as good looking as it is practical.

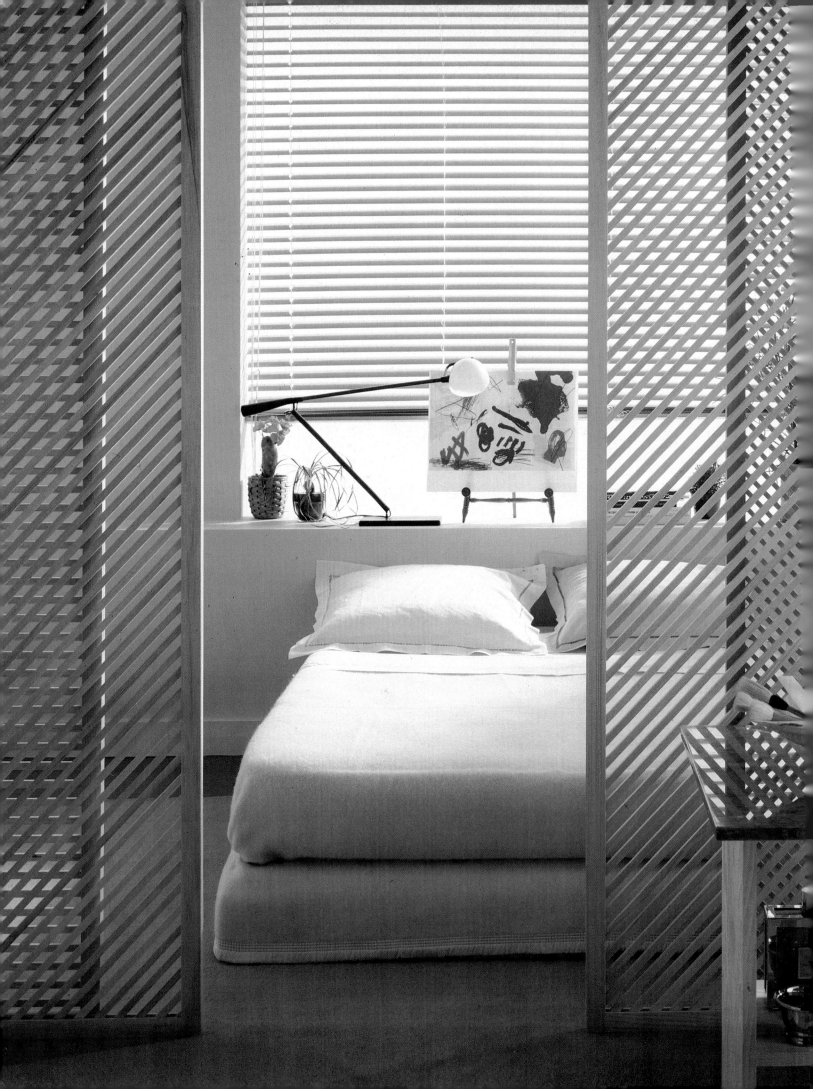

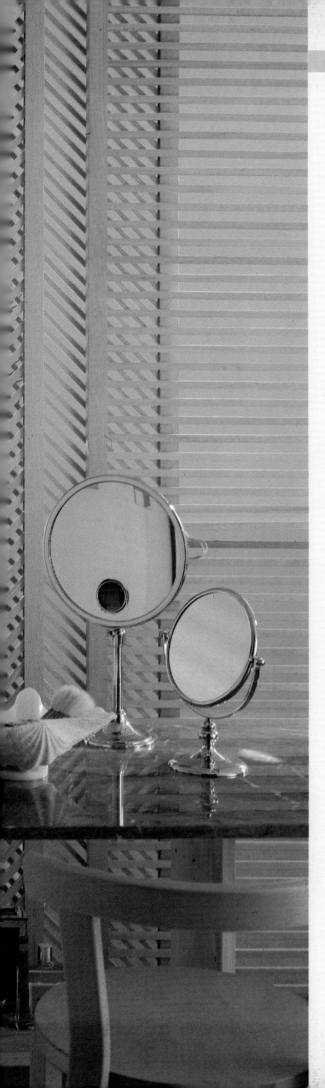

/// **W**hatever sort of house or apartment you rent or buy, it's a fair bet that you won't be a hundred percent happy about the space. Either you won't have enough of it or it will be arranged in a way that doesn't work for you. If it's a brand-new house or apartment, the chances are that the rooms are designed for modern living, i.e., well fitted out but tiny, and some of them, like the dining room, will have disappeared completely. You eat in the living room or the kitchen if it's big enough. The bathroom is minute; the bedrooms no more than little boxes. With older houses the space is there but never where you want it: a vast hall but no study or office; a walk-in pantry when you'd prefer a utility room.

You don't have to put up with it. Instead of adapting to the given space make it fit in with the way you want to live. Try to forget all the preconceived ideas about rooms and their conventional uses; see how the space can be changed around, expanded, reassessed. Look at every square inch and calculate the potential. Is there dead space – behind doors, for instance – that can be freed? Figure out how to use the walls, the space under the windows, how to open up confined areas, how to create impressions of space with light and color. Don't simply accept the space which you have been given; rethink it with a detailed and critical eye until you have exactly what you want.

Multi-purpose rooms often need some form of divider or screen to identify or conceal different areas. This floor-to-ceiling slatted screen has several plus points: it not only effectively separates the sleeping area from the rest of the room, its attractive thin diagonal slats allow in filtered light from the window.

One large room broken into different areas using a series of slatted blinds (right) is often better than a maze of small rooms. The roof supports have been cleverly incorporated into the scheme and painted blue to match the spiral staircase.

A small, cramped house (below) has been completely opened up on the ground floor. A low half-wall now provides the break between kitchen and dining room. An open staircase, once in a dark corridor, provides valuable storage space.

If removing a partition in a home that you own (you can't do this in rented housing) would create more space, then it's sensible to do it. Taking down non-load-bearing walls is a much cheaper operation than putting them up, and it opens up the space miraculously. Here are some well-tried and obvious ways that are very successful: an archway and 'window' opening in a blank hall/living room wall to let in light and create a sense of perspective; removing the wall between living room/dining room (especially applicable in a Victorian building, to make one large bright room instead of two dark cramped ones); and using half of a too-spacious hall and half of a useless passage to produce a reasonably sized kitchen that will allow more space for food preparation and, possibly, a small dining area, most useful for breakfast and casual meals.

Larger houses with good sized rooms can sometimes also benefit from having a few walls knocked down. The extra space for seating (above) gives an elegant room the fine proportions it needs to set off a series of magnificent floor-to-ceiling windows. Creating a handsome arch between the two rooms enhances the effect, while carpeting right through gives a feeling of continuity.

Another tiny house (left) has been opened up completely on the ground floor to create an all-in-one family living area, incorporating the extra light space of the hall: now a piano makes a natural divider between living area and front door, while a metal pole storage unit screens the kitchen area and provides the perfect place for a sofa. There is even room for a child's swing.

If you want to appear to double the size of the room and increase the amount of light at the same time, mirrors will do the trick. And they are a trick but one that is most effective.

A whole wall of mirrors is stunning, making it look as if you could walk right through to another room altogether. Mirroring from baseboard to ceiling in

Halls and bedrooms can often do with a little more space, and long mirrored doors on cabinets and closets are ideal for combining valuable storage with the illusion of a bigger room. An interesting or light reflection is essential as the two rooms right and far left demonstrate so effectively.

the recesses on either side of a fireplace will give you the same illusion and highlight what is a feature of the room.

Mirroring reflects every scrap of light by day and night, and by setting it up at right angles to a window wall, you reflect the window as well. And you do get the feeling of owning far more space than you actually have.

Creating an illusion of space without major structural upheavals or spending too much money is very important if you're short of cash or if you're in rented housing, where alterations to the structure are out of the question. When you can't make any changes in the amount or layout of square footage, the situation calls for even more careful consideration of the full range of possibilities to achieve a better feeling of spaciousness.

For instance, using large slabs of mirroring can be expensive so go for cheaper versions. Mirror tiles are a good substitute at half the price. Or you could stick up thin strips of mirroring at the top of the room just below the ceiling like a moulding or cornice. More simply, and cheaply, use a very large mirror, framed or unframed, opposite a window or on any wall that could take added sparkle.

A good way to get a huge handsomely framed mirror for very little money is to find an old picture frame in a junk shop, clean it up, re-gild if necessary with gold paint and buy a piece of mirror to fit. Mirrors sold for closet doors at your local home improvement store are often surprisingly inexpensive. Hang them side by side if you want to create a really special effect.

Mirror tiles can be just as effective as sheet mirror, particularly when divided by bands of primary color as they are here, to reflect the bright, modern furniture, which is perfectly in keeping with the style.

A shiny surface will often serve the same purpose as a mirrored one, catching reflections and bouncing the light around. The glossy light blue of this kitchen area helps it to look clean and bright, with lots of glass, chrome and shiny plastic to complete the illusion of light and space.

VISUAL CHEATING

If mirroring is impractical, expensive or not to your taste, very shiny walls can help. They will reflect light and seem much less solid and constricting. Plain light walls will produce a greater illusion of space than patterned ones, although a wallpaper with a geometric design against a white background will give a three-dimensional effect. Again, even the slight suggestion of perspective will make the walls appear less confining.

Foldaway mesh dining chairs can be quickly and easily hung on sturdy wall pegs when not in use – a real spacesaver.

Clean lines and a simple color scheme help generate a feeling of light and space. Note the plain white paper blind and fireplace.

Reflective surfaces catch the light and create the illusion of extra space: glass, mirrors, shiny metal and gloss paint.

Good lighting eliminates any dark gloomy corners. Here a strip of tiny bulbs behind a valance runs around the room.

Sofa bed and table back-to-back define the room's separate areas: one for eating and working, the other for sitting and sleeping.

Storage facilities need to look good if they are on display. Shelves showcase favorite items; window seat and boxes hide the rest.

Painted fiberboard columns make inexpensive but dramatic room dividers, with cutout shelves to provide extra storage.

One-room living can be stylish if you plan it carefully and use the space wisely. Every square inch, every corner must earn its keep if it is to provide a pleasant environment to eat, sleep, sit and even entertain. In many ways the less you start with the better off you are: furniture can be improvised to fit the shape and purpose of the room or chosen for its durability. Sofas fold out into double beds; tables are used that are large enough to serve as really practical worktops or to accommodate several dinner guests.

Visual tricks are important, too, making a room look larger than it really is or helping define the different areas with clever use of color and positioning of furniture. The designer of this room has gone one step further by installing two cylindrical room dividers, cleverly improvised from two fiberboard tubes manufactured for casting concrete columns. When they have been painted a smart, glossy gray and yellow and fitted with shelves, they make perfect visual dividers.

A light, bright color scheme always makes the most of a room's size; here mirrored recesses help the illusion with stripped and varnished floorboards stained a soft gray to match.

Making the most of what you have means using every corner imaginatively. This window seat was built from sturdy plywood with a hinged lid to allow the base to be used for storage of bulky items such as bed linen and pillows.

Running almost the length of one wall and neatly turning the corner into an alcove, it provides useful extra seating for dinner guests when the table is moved over, and with plenty of comfortable cushions, a cosy place to sit or stretch out too.

The base has been painted gray in order to match the walls. Predrilled mirror sections between glass shelves in the recess are a clever alternative to large, expensive sheet mirror and give the illusion of more space.

*T*he chameleon multipurpose room needs to change its mood with the passing of the hours. Flexible lighting is essential for switching emphasis to a different area and maybe creating a more intimate atmosphere. Here good general lighting is backed up with lights and lamps to meet specific purposes: a smart angular table lamp makes a good desk lamp during the day; by night it moves to the bedside for a little light reading. Dinner guests can enjoy their food in an atmosphere created by the flickering light of gas fireplaces and candles placed on what was the desk.

It is fascinating how the room quickly becomes either a bedroom, once the bed is made, or a dining room when the table is set. Coordinating colors and styles insure that each purpose area fits the room as a whole: smart geometric gray and yellow bed linen for example, black, gray and yellow for chairs, china and cutlery and the small extras – yellow candles and matching napkins.

Folding mesh chairs are ideal for dining, with padded tie-on seat cushions for extra comfort.

Simple table will seat four or even six guests comfortably and doubles as a large work surface during the day. It folds away completely if required.

Shelves fitted inside the tubular columns are ideal for storing books and dishes right to the ceiling in a very limited space. A small light fixture concealed at the top of each shelf creates an attractive illuminated effect and focuses attention on the dining area rather than the seating beyond.

Those final finishing touches turn a meal into something festive and need not be expensive. Coordinated table linen and china was achieved by keeping to a simple scheme of black, white and gray. Candles and napkins provide a bright splash of yellow to match chair and tube. The napkins match the cushions on the window seat and were made using the fabric remnants.

As the bed folds easily out of the sofa, the seating area quickly converts to a bedroom. Pillows and bed linen are stored inside the window seat unit and have been carefully chosen to match the general scheme of the room. The table, desk and dining table by day, immediately becomes a handy bedside surface between the two cylindrical columns and a convenient means of screening the bed from the rest of the room and window beyond. The blind is effective but inobtrusive.

If required, it is quite a simple task to mount the tubes on turntables which enable them to swivel and display their illuminated shelves on the reverse side. As well as providing a room divider, the tubes add height and distinction.

Carts are a one-room dweller's godsend. This handsome black model has three shelves ideal for moving hi-fi equipment, drinks or whatever to wherever they are needed in the room, but it would be equally suitable as a bedside table.

Lighting can change a room beyond recognition. Properly controlled, arranged and directed light can produce dramatic effects, bringing certain parts of the room forward, letting other areas recede or blur. Natural light, for example filtered through blinds or shades, will give a room subtlety which in itself will seem to diffuse the space. Harsh, bright light will create hard, sharply defined blocks of light and shadow; softer light will allow all the separate elements in the room to merge and become indistinct as a result.

Put uplights into corners and behind sofas, armchairs or plants to cast light on the ceiling which is then thrown back into the room. The whole room seems filled with light and shade and because the boundaries and edges of objects within the room are blurred the space seems endless.

SPECIAL EFFECTS

Set downlights or wallwashers into the ceiling, about 3 feet from the wall, if there is enough recess, or mount them on the ceiling, and they will literally bathe the walls with light; again, this has the effect of making any hard edges seem to disappear and expands the limits.

Get rid of any harsh overhead light from the middle of the ceiling. It does nothing for the room and doesn't give light where it's wanted. Take down the central fixture and plaster over it or, if you can't change it, just don't use it. Replace it with reading lamps positioned to throw light where it is needed on work or books and also to provide movable pools of light around the room – this is not only far more practical than a single ceiling fixture, but also more attractive and flattering.

If the cost of light fixtures is beyond you, make your own, though it must be said that some of the best, most imaginative and inexpensive lighting is to be found at the chain stores these days. It's hardly worth trying to improvise or invent effective directional lighting because there are so many good and reasonably priced clip-on spots or work lamps on the market. These can be clamped to furniture – table edges and so on – and adjusted to shine wherever you want.

Discover the dimmer. It's the best thing that has happened to lighting since Edison invented the light bulb. It brings sophisticated lighting within everybody's reach. If you can't afford any other sort at least install dimmers and try to have as many lights as possible working off them. The variations they give are enormous, altering the intensity of light, changing the look and mood of a room. Unfortunately, there is no way of doing this inexpensively; but should you decide to try them, when you see the scope they give you to alter whole rooms at a time, with the slightest touch, you may well decide it was one of the better investments you have made in decorating terms.

Look on lighting not as a static and fairly prosaic means of seeing when it's dark but more as theatrical special effect: a lovely flexible medium that you can experiment with and manipulate to show off every part of your house to its best advantage. By flooding with light that comes from all corners of the room or darkening right down to one spotlit object – and all the stages in between – you can disguise faults, emphasize good points and play clever tricks with the space which you have at your disposal. In other words, you will be in control of the situation and not a victim of it.

The combined kitchen/ dining room is often a difficult room to light because bright light is required for safe and pleasant cooking, but a more subtle effect is preferred for dining. An adjustable pendant type of lamp is the ideal solution.

A plain, light-colored wall is perfect for bouncing light into the rest of the room and creates a far subtler effect than a direct spotlight which tends to glare and dazzle. This room has been kept deliberately understated with very little decoration and simply styled furniture.

LIGHTING

As homeowners become increasingly aware of the importance of good lighting, the choice of fixtures has become wider and more attractive every year. Today there are a great many types and styles to suit every purpose – and every pocket – as the more stylish and imaginative designs filter down into the chain stores and department stores. There are all kinds of ingenious clips, racks and other fittings specially designed for lamps and spotlights, as well as freestanding uplights and downlights in a wide range of sizes. Choosing is simply a matter of identifying your lighting needs, then selecting the style you like to suit the purpose. Some lights are more flexible than others (swivelling, retracting, bending, or operable by remote control) and will serve several purposes; others are specially suited for outdoors or steamy bathrooms.

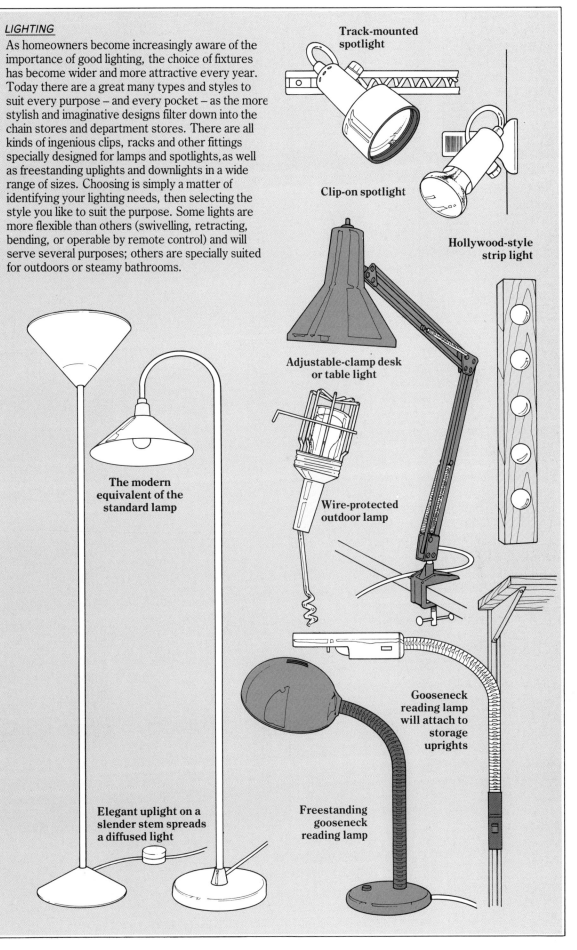

Track-mounted spotlight

Clip-on spotlight

Hollywood-style strip light

Adjustable-clamp desk or table light

Wire-protected outdoor lamp

The modern equivalent of the standard lamp

Gooseneck reading lamp will attach to storage uprights

Elegant uplight on a slender stem spreads a diffused light

Freestanding gooseneck reading lamp

SPACE-SAVERS – A QUICK GUIDE

/ / / Have two small sofas rather than four chairs – compact and stylish.

/ / / Push two small seating units together; they take up less room than two individual chairs spaced apart.

/ / / Concentrate storage along one wall; this makes maximum use of space and is neater than separate desks, shelves and cabinets scattered about the room.

/ / / Concentrate the TV, stereo, video equipment, records, cassettes in one place; it looks impressive and well organized.

/ / / Collect all your books together in one place; give them a whole wall of shelving. It will have more impact on the room and save space.

/ / / Use corners – often wasted space – as much as possible for beds, desks, cabinets, dressers, wardrobe units.

/ / / Line big pieces of furniture, such as bookcases, up against a wall.

/ / / Build in furniture wherever possible: shelves, cabinets, a whole wall's length of seating, storage under window seats – this will keep clutter under control and provide extra seating without the unfortunate necessity of sacrificing all available extra space.

/ / / Use fold-up furniture, such as casual chairs and tables, that can be stacked neatly away when not required, either in a large closet or hung up on an outsize hook on the wall.

/ / / Choose see-through furniture that can be stacked neatly away when not required, either in a large closet or hung up on an outsize hook on the wall.

/ / / Choose see-through tables and desks made of acrylic or glass or surfaced with mirrors. Because they don't block out light as solid wood or plastic would do, in effect, they appear to take up less room.

/ / / Have two good day beds rather than a bulky double bed if you live in a one-room apartment.

They won't dominate the room so much, and they can be piled with pillows by day to provide comfortable seating and pushed together again at night to form one large bed.

/ / / Build closets around a double bed so that an already small room won't seem overly full of furniture.

/ / / Restrict furniture to an absolute minimum if both money and space are limited. Make sure the few pieces you do choose are not only attractive but can stand a lot of wear and tear and need only a minimum of maintenance.

Shelving is an excellent space-saver if it makes good use of any odd corners or recesses. If you can't afford custom-built shelves and cabinets, put up cheap shelf-and-bracket units bought to size to fill gaps under the stairs, either side of the chimney breast or other recesses.

MAKE A PROPER ROOM PLAN

Once you've improved the sense of spaciousness by good decoration and lighting, keep it that way by paying careful attention to the size, amount and arrangement of furniture. If you're starting from scratch buying furniture, you can save yourself endless mistakes by making a room plan. It will help you to work out the number and approximate sizes of furniture and where they will fit in. Even if you're not yet at the actual buying stage you can work it all out in theory, juggling the pieces around on paper in different arrangements until you come up with the most satisfactory ones. A proper room plan drawn to scale should include positions of electrical outlets, radiators, breaks in the wall and all openings. This makes it useful for a contractor, if you're hiring one, or furniture movers. A good diagram (see below) is worth a hundred words.

When the room plan is finished, draw to scale on a piece of colored or plain cardboard any furniture that you own already. If you're at the buying stage, measure the furniture in the shop before you actually make any decision; then come home, cut out the pieces to scale and move them around on your room plan until you're happy about the position. Identify each piece – 'armchair', 'table' and so on. If you're not ready to buy, make a note of the room measurements and have this handy when you go comparison shopping for furniture so that you can do an approximate check for suitability while actually in the store.

Once you have some or all of the pieces cut to scale it's simply a matter of playing with them, moving them about in various positions until you see which arrangement is the most feasible. You have to remember traffic routes, focal points like fireplaces, electrical sockets, lighting positions and radiators; these will all affect the way you finally place the furniture. With limited space this really is the most practical and sensible approach.

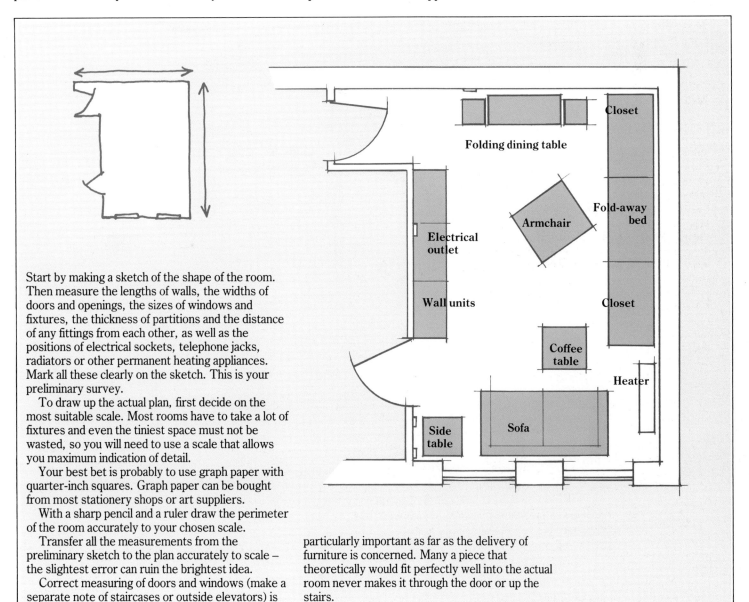

Start by making a sketch of the shape of the room. Then measure the lengths of walls, the widths of doors and openings, the sizes of windows and fixtures, the thickness of partitions and the distance of any fittings from each other, as well as the positions of electrical sockets, telephone jacks, radiators or other permanent heating appliances. Mark all these clearly on the sketch. This is your preliminary survey.

To draw up the actual plan, first decide on the most suitable scale. Most rooms have to take a lot of fixtures and even the tiniest space must not be wasted, so you will need to use a scale that allows you maximum indication of detail.

Your best bet is probably to use graph paper with quarter-inch squares. Graph paper can be bought from most stationery shops or art suppliers.

With a sharp pencil and a ruler draw the perimeter of the room accurately to your chosen scale.

Transfer all the measurements from the preliminary sketch to the plan accurately to scale – the slightest error can ruin the brightest idea.

Correct measuring of doors and windows (make a separate note of staircases or outside elevators) is particularly important as far as the delivery of furniture is concerned. Many a piece that theoretically would fit perfectly well into the actual room never makes it through the door or up the stairs.

This room is a masterly attempt at one-room living – and working. The desk serves as efficient room divider and doubles as a dining table, while the bed is used for seating during the day. The two areas are lucky enough to have a window apiece which helps emphasize their separateness. Storage for books, clothes and other possessions has been cleverly built in around the room and there is even a little kitchen area hidden behind a blind.

Every room has to earn its keep and with careful planning some can be made to do double if not triple duty. A dining room, for instance, which is only used as such at certain set times of the day and would otherwise be standing idle, can act as a home office/study. If it can take a sofa bed you have a potential short-stay guest room as well. If there's a wall of storage units set one drawer aside for clothes; or a wooden hat stand could be pressed into service for hanging clothes on – it wouldn't look out of place in a dining room and is better than putting a hook on the door. A good clamp light can be brought in for homework, study or for the use of an overnight guest who needs a bedside light.

Bedrooms, too, normally out of use all day, can be offices/studies/work rooms. The simplest and most space-efficient arrangement is to build a run of filing cabinets or chests of drawers under a window or along a wall, leaving kneehole space and topping them with laminated plastic wood which is easy to clean and tough enough not to be damaged by a typewriter. Add a mirror and you will have a useful and attractive dressing table as well.

UTILIZE YOUR WALLS

Fit a whole wall with freestanding, floor-to-ceiling self-assembly units to provide desk space and plenty of shelf and cabinet space. Just as reasonably priced are tubular metal shelving systems that can be built up in sections and provide very well organized work space. Hinged fold-down tables are wonderful space-savers and can turn a bedroom into a sewing room or hobby place and back again in no time to a room that gives no hint of its 'secret life'.

Adapt ideas from the kitchen and make use of wall grids, wire baskets and trays hung under shelves. Even in one room you can shut off a work corner with a screen, a desk and a lamp.

This study bedroom (above) has fitted inexpensive shelving and a desktop between a vertical half wall and the closet. Storage under the bed provides extra facilities. Industrial metal shelving (left) with a metal grid behind offers the chance to store and display a vast number of objects in a minimum space: an instant office or workroom which could be tucked in anywhere. A cubbyhole just big enough for a double bed (far left) is now a comfortable sleeping/seating area with plenty of storage.

The traditional study-library type den can be created in any style or size of house. This room was not only brand new and somewhat featureless, but also extremely small and had to double as spare bedroom for occasional guests. Built-in shelves and a sofa which unfolds to form a double bed solved the space problem; a rich red, green and blue theme was inspired by the traditional Turkish carpet.

The compact sofa bed is rich red piped in blue and opens out easily to provide a comfortable double bed complete with properly sprung mattress which folds up neatly inside when not needed. Shelving has been built around the window to provide ample storage for books in minimum space, with the desk slotted in under the window for maximum light during day-time. A thick green felt shade edged in braid at the window makes an effective screen where there is no room for curtains. A cosy intimate atmosphere is further enhanced by the use of matching green felt on the walls, a good sound deadener and insulation against the cold. The felt is stretched taut across the walls to provide a warm, textured surface and a gentleman's club atmosphere. Any good quality but not costly fabric can be used, although a strong plain color is probably best in such a small room.

Very often, a room set aside as study or workroom has to double as a spare bedroom. The sofa bed provides the ideal space-saving solution and is available in a wide range of styles – and prices. Do not buy the cheaper foam mattress type if the bed is to be slept on frequently as it will not withstand the wear. Most open out quickly and easily on a special mechanism allowing the mattress to be stored conveniently within the sofa structure. In this room, adjustable angled wall lights are not only perfect for reading when the sofa is in use, but make very good bedside lamps. Bed linen is stored in a built-in cabinet, its door also covered in green felt. The comforter cover and pillowcases are black and white stripe edged thinly in red.

If you are short of space, build shelves or cabinets along one wall or around the window for neat, economical storage. These are homemade using sturdy wood painted to match other woodwork in the room, but any adjustable shelving system could be used.

No room for desk space? This old desk with its hinged work-top provides the perfect surface for writing, reading, etc., although unsuitable for typewriters or sewing machines. It folds up neatly out of the way when the bed is in use and offers generous drawer storage.

In very small rooms you can afford to splash out on a more expensive floor covering. This Turkish carpet might seem an extravagance in a study/bedroom, but the actual floor area is so small, it becomes affordable. Look out for remnants and closeouts for small rooms too.

Small rooms can also take advantage of more unusual wall coverings. The green baize effect used here is perfect for that gentleman's club atmosphere and is available in fairly large widths. Almost any type of fabric can be used clipped to tracks, stapled to wooden cleats above and below, or hung like curtains on thin rods.

Lighting is so important to change the mood of a room and is doubly important where that room has more than one use. Wall lights cast a subtle, intimate glow yet are bright enough for reading if pulled closer to the bed or sofa. The window provides plenty of natural light for the desk area which also has an adjustable desk lamp for gloomy days and after dark.

Rented housing can be a dreary place that you can't do much about in terms of decorating or furnishing. This may be either because the landlord won't allow it or because if you're renting you aren't going to be there forever and you don't have money to spare anyway. Even if you did, it wouldn't be worthwhile spending too much only to profit the landlord or future tenants. Students in college rooms or housing, members of the armed forces and their families living in married quarters, hard-up newlyweds and the impecunious young generally are all faced with the same problem: how to turn temporary and usually unpromising rooms into a real home that is not only warm, comfortable and convenient to live, work and entertain in, but also interesting and reasonably attractive.

DECORATION MAKES A DIFFERENCE
Clever decoration can exaggerate limited space. Here are some simple ideas:

/ / / Use the same floor covering or treatment throughout a small house or apartment. If walls and ceiling are kept the same color as well, then the space will appear to flow on without interruption. If you think this is too monotonous, use subtle variations of the same color scheme from room to room.

/ / / Let light colors work for you. Pale shades recede while strong, intense, dark ones close in, so if you want a room to look bigger use light colors to push out the walls, stretch the floor space and heighten the ceiling.

/ / / If a small room has a high ceiling, paint it a darker color than the walls.

/ / / Go for diagonal stripes. They lead the eye away in to the distance so that the space seems both wider and longer. They are most effective used on the floor, either in a carpet or with striped composition flooring such as vinyl tiles or sheet vinyl or, least expensive of all, with stripes of paint.

/ / / Remove anything that breaks up a stretch of space. Either take down any picture rail or – more advisable in rented housing – make it vanish by painting it the same color as the walls.

/ / / Choose patterns carefully. Geometric designs or ones that seem to move in a certain direction and invite the eye to travel are good space stretchers on walls or flooring. Pattern on a white or light background will give a feeling of depth. Wallpaper with an all-over motif can look dense but if you have the same motif on a smaller scale for curtains, shades, covers, tablecloths, this will extend the space. A coordinated scheme of wallpaper and fabric lets the pattern loose all over the room but keeps it subtly controlled.

/ / / Take advantage of any good long view to be had from a window, or any sort of greenery that can be seen from inside. Let the room appear to melt into the view uninterrupted by curtains or furniture.

/ / / Use window shades instead of curtains.

/ / / Hang pictures on either side of a narrow room or corridor to widen the space.

Swathing the walls in lengths of fabric hung and gathered on rods or cleats will hide a multitude of sins, from crumbly plaster and damp stains to nasty wallpaper. Although this room is only small and serves as both sitting and dining room, it has a light, airy feel and an elegant atmosphere with the fabric continued across the patio doors in a classic twist.

INSTANT IMPROVEMENTS

/ / / Brighten the walls with pictures and posters. If you are not allowed to put nails or picture hooks in, hang your art from an old-fashioned picture rail; you can get special picture rail hanging clips. If there isn't one, create your own. Use an extendable spring-loaded rod, available from most photographic equipment shops. Hang everything from it with nylon line or even ribbon.

/ / / Change the wall color by using the same extendable rods, running them through a roll of seamless colored paper normally used for photographic backdrops. Pull down a new color whenever you fancy or the mood takes you at the flick of a wrist. (These rolls are available in a handsome range of colors.)

/ / / Hide hideous paint or wallpaper or give a fresh look to grubby walls with cheesecloth, an excellent and inexpensive temporary wall covering. Cut lengths to hang from ceiling to baseboards. (Or use traverse rods or extendable spring-loaded rods to secure the material top and bottom.) If you're just letting it hang loose, loop the cheesecloth back over doors, windows and cabinets and attach with thumbtacks if walls are reasonably soft; use small picture hooks if they're not. If you stretch the material tight you will need to secure it on either side of such openings, or for a neater finish, run cords or elastic or wire over the tops of doors and windows and suspend separate short lengths so that the undersurface will be totally hidden from view.

Zigzag wallpaper (left) helps broaden a narrow room. The theme is echoed in the black bands of floor tiles and an eye-catching pair of futon sofa beds in geometric fabric.

This room (below) looks much larger than it really is thanks to bold diagonal stripes leading the eye up and out. The subtle shades of gray are balanced by the use of other plain gray and black surfaces.

Small rooms can take a brave, dramatic scheme (left) where attention will be focused on style rather than size. Here, eye-catching tiles have been arranged on walls and floor in stripes and zigzags and balanced with large areas of pure, uninterrupted red.

Framed panels of coordinating wallpaper are guaranteed to liven up a plain papered wall at very little cost. Here the main color of the wallpaper design has been picked out and used to paint the frames and match the furniture.

This room is a master of disguise: a splendid mahogany screen displaying a rogues' gallery of portraits hides a pair of doors not quite in keeping with the rest of the room; a worn sofa is swiftly renewed with a length of fine fabric simply thrown over, while a small table crowded with favorite possessions draws the eye away from any flaws.

/ / / If you dislike the curtains but can't change them, take them down and substitute hanging baskets of plants; or buy the cheapest possible bamboo blinds which you can take with you when you leave. (They will almost certainly fit the window and if they are too big, can always be cut with a pair of sharp scissors.) Other inexpensive window treatments are window shades, which are available plain or in colorful patterns; pleated paper blinds; Indian bedspreads, which make beautiful curtains; yards and yards of cheesecloth or muslin – easily dyed – which can look sumptuous. Or you can buy excellent fabrics by the yard from good stores. Appropriate fabrics would be those that come in all cotton, polyester and cotton or a new crease-resistant 100 percent cotton. Choose from a good range of colors and from various widths. Such fabrics are generally reasonably priced and good value.

/ / / If the carpet is a horrible color, or very shabby, or both, buy whatever rugs you can afford. Look at them as an investment – if you move you can always find a place for them. Cover the worst of the color or the wear marks with them. There are excellent ranges of inexpensive, good looking rugs to be found in chain stores and department stores. If you're handy they are easy enough to make yourself but they take time, so be sure you want to spend your winter evenings with a rug kit before you lay out money for it.

/ / / If lighting is the usual unsubtle center fixture with the occasional lamp, then invest in one or two uplights and place them in corners behind plants and pieces of furniture. The difference will be remarkable. You can almost ignore the center light; only use it when absolutely necessary. Buy a small spotlight to pinpoint any treasures, photographs or attractive pictures. If you cannot afford a spot, buy a clip-on work lamp from a hardware store and attach that instead.

/ / / If you are allowed to paint but can't afford to do the whole room, try just painting the trims (baseboards, door and window frames, and any moldings) with a contrast color in semigloss. It will give an immediate lift to the look of a room.

/ / / Give instant glamour to a room by 'panelling it' out with strips of picture framing which can be bought in lengths in whatever style you like, and can afford, from most framers. All you have to do is stick it to the wall with any adhesive good for wood and plaster, in squares or rectangles worked out in proportion to the room. Draw the elevation of the room to scale on graph paper first, and then work out the design. Or, if you're confident enough, work it straight out on the walls with a long yardstick, light pencil and an eraser.

/ / / Add color, interest and lift to a room with plants. Buy the fullest and best shapes you can afford to make a definite statement. Stand them in corners, lit from behind with uplights or spots or a work lamp, mass them on windowsills, add them to arrangements of any kind of collection you may have, let them hang, trail and climb to create interest at different levels. The fresh, living green of well-kept foliage is one of the best decorative features you can have and will cheer up the dullest of rented rooms.

/ / / If small dashes and splashes of color are all you can afford, don't worry; they'll give a room warmth and personality. For this there's nothing better than throw pillows in attractive shades and designs. Use them to pull a dull scheme together and to liven up less than perfect upholstery which you can't change.

/ / / The more personal touches you can supply to furnished rented accommodation the better: an occasional chair in a solid color that picks up one of the other colors in the room, say from curtains or upholstery fabric; a screen to bring life to a dark corner – a mirrored screen will pay dividends in added light and sparkle and space; any small item of furniture like a needlework stool, clusters of photographs, pretty plates, accessories of any kind that help to give an individual touch. Group them carefully for deliberate impact; scattered about, even the most beautiful 'treasures' can become just messy clutter.

/ / / Put today's beautifully designed sheets and bed linen on show and you hardly need any other decoration in a bedroom. Dress up a bed with matching blanket covers, pillow shams, sheets and dust ruffles, piles of different-shaped lace or crocheted cushions and you have an immediate eye-catching centerpiece. Add to the effect with plain inexpensive round wooden tables covered with sheets or bedspreads; tuck the ends in underneath the table. Buy sets of bed linen more economically in white sales at department stores or from discount linen dealers, or buy seconds when they are available.

/ / / If you are allowed to make minor decorative changes and the existing scheme is in good condition but dull, cheer it up with an instant frieze or border. Buy yards of braid or colored tape, anything from 1 inch to 2½ inches wide, depending on the proportions of the room. Either run the braid or tape around the walls just below the ceiling and above the baseboard (stick it on, if it is not already adhesive-backed, with a suitable adhesive), or make the whole thing more elaborate by running it around doors and window frames as well, and down the corners too. It's easy enough to rip off before it dries permanently if you think you've overdone it.

Wallpaper borders can be used on plain painted walls in the same way as fabric trims. They are available in a wide range of widths and patterns and are generally less expensive than braid.

/ / / Stencil your own border or, even more ambitiously, garland motifs all over the walls. Stenciling kits are not expensive and it's great fun to do. Once you're into the swing of it you'll want to stencil everything – floors, furniture, fabrics.

A large, imposing room was given warmth and character with a minimum of effort. Fine molding and panelling were all painted white as an airy backdrop for a collection of fine plants – always effective space fillers – with chairs and sofa recovered in a pretty floral print to emphasize the summery feel. A peacock blue screen hides a cluttered desk.

/// The first thing that should be done in any room is to get the framework right – that is to say, before you can concentrate on the decoration and furnishings you must see that walls, ceiling, floor and windows are in a reasonable condition. To skimp on this would be false economy and a constant source of irritation. And the better you prepare a room the better the final result will be when you are in a position to decorate.

WALLS

Examine the walls. Are there any long deep cracks? Is the plaster sagging anywhere in walls or ceiling? Are there any nasty stains signalling missing tiles, bricks that need regrouting or a leaking pipe? Give the inside of the room as thorough an inspection as you did earlier on the outside. You might have to hire a professional to get things back into shape and cure the faults at the source unless you are handy yourself.

Dampness problems will require professional advice but condensation problems can be overcome by applying an undercoat of anticondensation paint to the walls or by superimposing plasterboard (attached to cleats or thin wooden uprights) over the old walls and treating it with preservative.

Shabby old plaster or plasterboard will need checking. If it is merely uneven or cracked, patch up the cracks with spackle, smooth them down with sandpaper and cover them with lining paper. If it is damp, you must first make sure that the cause is dealt with. You might get away with repairing just part of the plaster, but sometimes the whole wall might need to be stripped and replastered or replasterboarded. Remember that new plaster must be allowed to dry properly before any redecoration starts. Before painting, all walls should be sanded smooth and washed down with warm water and a bit of ammonia or household detergent.

Old paper can be painted over if it is still in good condition, but first make sure that its colors are fast. Try a small area; if the color runs, or if it is in poor condition, it will have to be stripped off, and the exposed underwall thoroughly washed to remove old size or paste.

Walls, floors and woodwork in good condition can afford to be treated simply. Here the walls have been painted a warm cream to complement natural duck seating and a plain wooden slatted shade. A ceramic tiled floor echoes the clean, simple lines but needs a good, level floor to be laid well. If yours is less than perfect, you may have to lay plywood first.

Old woodwork on doors, window frames and baseboards should be both washed and sanded, but if there are several layers of paint on it already, or if the paint is rough, it is advisable to strip it all off because any new paint might chip.

If papering, use heavy lining paper, hung *horizontally,* and butt edges together smoothly.

Time and effort spent on preparation is never wasted; on the contrary it makes the actual decoration go far more smoothly. Without it new paintwork would discolor and new paper peel.

HANGING LINING PAPER

Cut your lengths of lining paper to fit the wall horizontally, allowing a generous overlap. Paste as you would wallpaper, folding into manageable sections as you go.

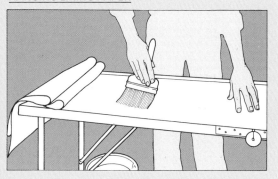

Apply the paper to the wall horizontally, unfolding as you go along and smoothing with the flat of your hand, taking care not to stretch or snag the paper. Use a level to make sure the first piece is hung straight.

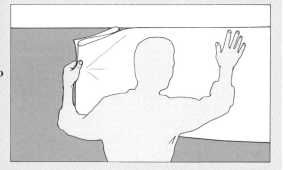

As you continue to apply the paper to the wall, smooth out any creases or bubbles using a wallpaper brush, keeping a firm hold on the rest of the paper to prevent it from sagging or tearing.

When you reach the corner, take your length of lining paper around and press into the corner using the edge of a wallpaper scraper. Trim as required and start your next length, remembering to butt the edges.

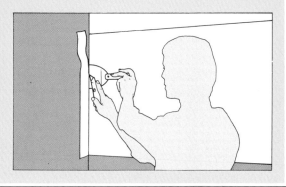

WHAT GOES ON THE WALLS?

Once the walls are ready to work on you have to decide how to cover them. The choice is basically between paint, paper and fabric. What you actually choose depends on how much you want to spend and the type of area you are covering.

Painting is the easiest and most economical way of transforming a room. Some other form of wallcovering that would look better for longer might work out more cheaply in the long run, but for an immediate good effect paint is excellent. And if you prefer plain walls in living rooms and bedrooms, it's the obvious answer. Major traffic areas like halls and stairways, however, might require tougher surfaces – especially if you have children.

If you do decide on paint and find yourself vacillating about the color, there's a lot to be said for white. If the room is small and dark, if it's rented, or if you just want to play it absolutely safe, white is the perfect solution. It's practical, neutral and easy to live with. It will flatter the shape of a room, make it

look lighter, neater, airier. It's an excellent background for all sorts of possessions and for vivid splashes of color from pillows, rugs, pictures, flowers. Practically anything looks good against white. There's nothing like it for producing a complete transformation; it's acceptable to landlords and, if you are not sure at the start about the exact effect you are trying to achieve, then white walls will give you a breathing space and look attractive while you are making a decision about what you want the final color to be.

Recently, paint manufacturers have been falling over themselves to produce ranges of whites faintly flushed with color – pale apple white, rose-tinged white, blue white, straw-tinted white. This gives you the merest suggestion of color. Even if you still keep the walls dead white you could paint the woodwork and ceiling in a tinted shade. Such very subtle differences not only look extremely elegant, but they also make the final effect more interesting than plain white throughout.

Plenty of white paint can make a room look twice the size it really is and offers an easy inexpensive option if you like plain walls. But white needn't mean a stark and colorless scheme with the wide range of tinted whites available these days. The lovely country-style sitting room (top left) is painted white with a soft and soothing touch of barley brown; the fresh dining room (top right) has been enlivened by a slight hint of green; the hallway (left) has a welcoming pink blush that adds warmth.

An unashamedly romantic bedroom like this may look terrifically expensive but can, in fact, be achieved quite economically. The walls and windows have been draped in inexpensive muslin fabric, gathered on stretched wires and pulled back with colored ribbons. Inexpensive plywood tables have been disguised with floorlength cloths and the bed scattered with plenty of ruffled, romantic cushions.

The floor has been simply sanded, stained and varnished and topped with a pastel rag rug for bedside comfort. Fresh flowers are a final indulgence. It is a look that could easily be copied in a bedroom of any size or shape.

Muslin or cheesecloth is inexpensive to buy by the yard and does a great job of covering up uneven walls or providing temporary decoration while creating a sumptuous boudoir effect. It should be cut to length and hemmed top and bottom then threaded on stretched wires like those used to hang sheer curtains. Allow twice the wall's width for fullness. Alternatively, the fabric can be stapled to thin strips of wood, but it is more difficult to remove for cleaning purposes without damaging it.

Another effect which can be achieved with fabric is to use a more expensive printed design instead of wallpaper – useful for rented housing – either fastened flat to wood strips with padding behind or hemmed and gathered on poles for a pleated effect.

Lengths of muslin drawn back from the window have been echoed over the bed to create an almost half-tester effect. With a pretty flower print in the center, it makes a really special feature of what is already a fine brass bed.

Satin ribbons in different pastel shades, reflected in those of the throw pillows, have been used to tie back the muslin and emphasize the room's feminine charms.

A pile of frilly pillows and throw pillows on plain white ruffled bed linen make any room immediately more romantic. These are coordinated with the pale pastel printed shade at the window.

The floor has been stripped, sanded and varnished for a warm, mellow effect against the stark white of the rest of the scheme. For a slightly different effect, stain with walnut or mahogany shades or stencil with flowers in a border pattern.

Bedside tables covered in plain and patterned cloths are not just attractive but big enough for a pair of soft pink lamps, clock and bedtime reading matter. The tables beneath can be as scuffed as you please provided they are stable.

A large oak chest at the foot of the bed brings the room down to earth with a practical bump: the surface is useful for books and flowers and it also offers storage for pillows, bed linen and bulky sweaters.

A bedside rug prevents cold feet in the mornings if you can't afford wall-to-wall carpeting. This one is based on the old traditional rag rug techniques where fabric was torn into strips and reused woven into rugs. A pastel dhurrie would also have looked good.

Stencilling and marbling are just two of the many decorative paint finishes that have been revived lately. Until recently such effects were the province of the grand decorators or old village craftsmen but now anyone who is handy and can paint should be able to follow all the newly publicized instructions for stencilling, marbling, glazing, rag rubbing, stippling, and dragging. These very gentle effects, softly blurring colors into each other, make an enormous difference to a room; because of the 'texture' created the main effect is to introduce lots of interesting light and shade, enlivening what might otherwise be a flat, dead surface.

You can now buy very good stencilling kits at reasonable prices from either stationery or art supply and craft shops. Once you've got the hang of it you can progress to making your own motifs, repeating say, a carpet or tile design or something from folk art or a fabric that would lend itself to simple repetition.

Most of the other paint finishes make use of glazing liquid which you can buy from specialist paint stores. It's a thickish cream which needs thinning down with mineral spirits or paint thinner and mixing with a tint or artist's oil paint to get exactly the right shade. When it is brushed or rubbed on over an opaque oil-based matte base, it forms a transparent film or color. The base must be painted in oil paint because if a latex paint were used, it would simply absorb the glaze and the whole elaborately applied effect would disappear completely.

GETTING THAT GLAZED LOOK

To tint a glaze you'll need a suitable choice of artists' oil paints from an art shop, a couple of old saucepans or large containers or some of those deep foil food dishes, turpentine or mineral spirits and, finally, a spoon and an old cup.

Squeeze an inch or so of paint into one of the containers and stir in several tablespoons of the turpentine or spirits; mix thoroughly until smooth, then add about a cup of glazing liquid and mix together thoroughly.

Test the mixture out on a board – or the wall if you feel confident – and have a large supply of clean rags to rub it off afterward. If the mixture needs strengthening or changing, mix a bit more tint in another pan, add the glaze as before and test again. Go on doing this until you have achieved the right mix but don't be tempted to mix the paint straight into the glaze in order to save time – because it won't work.

You can simply glide this magic glaze over a given color in either the same shade or a darker one or you can experiment with other techniques like stippling, dragging, or rag rolling. It takes time and elbow grease but for a very low cost you end up with beautiful walls with the sort of delicate textured look that you usually only get from expensive hand

Hallways which are so often neglected or doomed to unimaginative or boring treatment, are excellent candidates for some exciting paint effects. The interesting or unpredictable makes a good entrance to your home: the rag-rolled walls (left) incorporating a low, plain border draw the eye toward some fine stencilling on floor and stairs, applied in a most unobvious way, while the hallway (above) has created a fanciful domestic landscape in pastel colors.

SMART AS PAINT

You can do all sorts of clever things with paint. For instance:

/ / / Make a low ceiling seem higher by painting it a lighter color than the walls.

/ / / Make a high room seem better proportioned by painting a dado all around the walls. Do this by attaching a length of molding at chair height, paint it in with the rest of the woodwork and paint the space below a contrasting shade.

/ / / Give character and interest to featureless rooms with simple but imaginative color treatment: keep walls and woodwork in a light color and paint a band or two bands of color all around the room just under the ceiling; or paint graduated bands of color in different widths, starting from the baseboard and working up.

/ / / Disguise eyesores like unsightly pipes, off-center doors or windows, irregular ceiling levels, ugly radiators, by painting everything a warm, dark color. Alternatively brazen it out by actually drawing attention to such features, picking them out in a stunning color as if they were sculptural objects.

/ / / Bring a very ordinary room to life by painting doors and windows a bright primary color – yellow, green, bright red – again keeping walls white or a light color.

/ / / Paint stencil borders or motifs on walls; they look attractive and are right in fashion. Or try a different kind of border by painting diagonal stripes on baseboards in an otherwise plain room. Or 'marble' them – more subtle, very sophisticated and back in favor again.

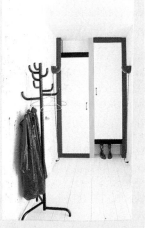

Colors make their best impact when part of an overall scheme. Bright pink and yellow (left) look young and fresh; primaries (above) are strong against white.

Stencilling can add interest to the smallest of rooms. This tiny bathroom has combined both border and picture stencils with a floral theme against a background of rag-rolled walls and ceiling. It is a clever treatment for a sloping, uneven room, often so difficult to tackle.

printing. Since practice makes perfect here, it's wise to experiment first on pieces of board that have been sized, then given an undercoat of oil paint followed by a coat of oil-based matte in exactly the same color as the one you've chosen for your walls. This practice period will give you time in which to develop a feeling of confidence in using the technique and in the colors you can produce.

The walls will need sealing with a final coat or coats of polyurethane, which comes in matte, semigloss or high gloss and can be put on with a roller. Follow up by brushing out any bubbles with a soft, clean brush before they dry and harden and so ruin the whole effect. This last finishing touch of polyurethane will give a wall a handsome sheen, but it tends to darken the tone slightly and you should allow for this. Try to buy one that is as clear as possible and if you are going to put on more than one coat, you should wait at least 24 hours between each

application. The more coats of polyurethane you add, the harder and tougher the final finish and, a most important consideration, the longer the walls will stay looking good.

HOW MUCH PAINT?

You can work out how much paint you need for a room by multiplying the number of feet or yards around a room by the height. One gallon of paint will give a base or first coat of around 60 square yards. New plaster or plasterboard might well need more because it will absorb the paint, so in that case allow 1 gallon for every 40 square yards. Successive coats will, of course, require less.

You will find that glazing liquid goes farther than paint: ½ pint of glaze will generally cover about 60 square feet; 1 quart will cover around 250 square feet; and one gallon of glaze will cover around 1,000 square feet.

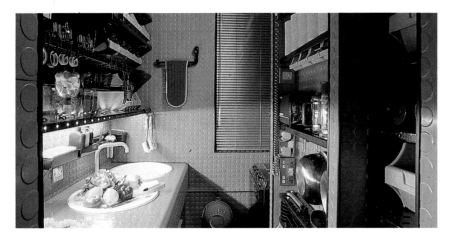

WALLCOVERINGS

The range of wallpapers these days is almost overwhelming – and not just more but better. Designer wallpapers are now available at discount prices so if you yearn for the lovely patterns you see in the glossy magazines you'll find there's a good choice even for lean budgets.

If you admire the painted finishes described above but can't tackle them yourself there are papers with marbled, dragged, and rag-rolled effects that will be indistinguishable from the real thing, especially if given a sealing coat of polyurethane. They tend to be expensive so why not use them in a very small room, like a bathroom, small hall or study, which

Strong color can work in a confined space. This tiny galley kitchen has been easily and inexpensively transformed by covering every surface in durable bright green vinyl flooring material with a stud effect. Touches of yellow and red have been chosen for trim and accessories.

CALCULATING WALLPAPER QUANTITIES

Wallpaper should be very carefully calculated before you buy. Apart from the fact that it is extremely annoying either to have expensive rolls left over or to run out, wallpaper should always be bought from the same printing batch (indicated by a number on the wrapper) to avoid any mis-matches of color or pattern. To work out exactly how many rolls you need, measure the room carefully, both height and width, remembering to take into account any alcoves or irregularities. Follow the chart below, bearing in mind that if the paper has a pattern, the larger it is, the more you will need for matching. It is important to bear in mind that wallpapers from smaller, more unusual companies may be of non-standard lengths.

AMERICAN WALLPAPERS
Table for calculating number of rolls required

Feet around room	Height of wall in feet					
	8	9	10	11	12	14
28	7	8	9	10	11	12
36	9	10	11	12	13	16
44	11	12	14	15	16	19
52	13	15	16	18	19	22
60	15	17	19	20	22	26
68	17	19	21	23	25	29
72	18	20	22	24	27	31
80	20	22	25	27	30	34
88	22	24	27	30	32	38
92	23	26	28	31	34	39
96	24	27	30	32	35	41

IMPORTED WALLPAPERS
Table for calculating number of rolls required

Feet around room	Height of wall in feet						
	7-7½	7½-8	8-8½	8½-9	9½-10	10-10½	10½-11½
28	4	4	4	4	5	5	5
32	4	4	5	5	6	6	6
40	5	5	6	6	7	7	7
44	6	6	7	7	7	8	8
52	7	7	8	8	9	9	9
56	7	8	8	9	9	10	10
60	8	8	9	9	10	10	11
64	8	9	9	10	10	11	11
68	9	9	10	10	11	12	12
72	9	10	11	11	12	12	13
80	10	11	12	12	13	14	14
84	10	11	12	13	14	14	15

would only need a few rolls. Many of them come with coordinating borders or friezes which add a professional finishing touch. A less expensive way of achieving the same look is to use narrow grosgrain or velvet ribbon, backed with an appropriate adhesive just under the ceiling or cornice and around doors and windows if you like. Or cut your own border from a roll of paper with a linear design that will go with the background paper.

If you fall in love with an impossibly expensive paper and want to use it in a large room, try putting it up in panels. One roll might be enough if you cut it into equal rectangles in proportion to your walls and paste it up on a background painted the same color as the background of the paper. Finish off by nailing thin wood molding or beading around the panels, mitering the corners. The molding could be painted either to coordinate with the walls or to contrast with the paper.

Inexpensive wallpaper with a good design can be made to look much more expensive and to last much longer with two coats of polyurethane. Wait at least 24 hours between coats. The paper should be tested first for color-fastness. If the color holds, the polyurethane should make it tough enough to be used in a bathroom.

If you like the texture and look of burlap on walls, but don't like the price, an acceptable substitute is the canvas used by painters or the kind that is sold to go under needlepoint. This could be either stuck up carefully (spreading the paste first on the walls, not the canvas), or stapled and then given a coat or two of paint.

Another good idea is to use the sort of seamless paper that photographers put up for backgrounds. Already recommended for easy facelifts in rented homes, it is a splendid way of getting very quick changes for those who are easily bored. The paper comes in a large range of colors and a variety of widths from photographers' supply shops. It can be hung from spring-loaded tension rods mounted just below the ceiling, or from rods cut to size and mounted on brackets. The bottom of the paper should be weighted with a wooden dowel or a section of narrow plumber's piping.

ORDERING WALLPAPER

Most dealers will help you work out how much wallpaper you need if you tell the size of your room, i.e. height and length of walls. Both imported and domestic wallpapers come in standard roll sizes (see chart). Always order an extra roll or two in case of mistakes – batches might differ.

For your guidance, a useful table of room sizes is shown opposite, giving the number of standard rolls needed, in both imported and American sizes, for varying heights and sizes of rooms. You should deduct one roll of wallpaper for every two doors or windows in the room.

Decorating ideas can be a lot more flexible than you think. Door panels can be painted in coordinating colors or even papered to match your walls (left); while plain pleated window shades (below) make an unusual versatile wall-covering.

The way you paint the woodwork in a room can make a good deal of difference in the effect you are trying to achieve. You can either go for contrast by painting it white or off-white, or have a much quieter look by painting it the same color as the walls but using either gloss or semigloss paint so that it can be easily cleaned. Or you can create something much more interesting by giving baseboards a fancy finish of dragging or marbling. You can do the same for door and window frames. Because these are very confined areas it calls for quite a lot of skill. It is important to remember to be patient and work slowly – but steadily – as possible. The finished effect is all-important and you cannot afford to let it be less than perfect.

An easier way of pepping up ordinary paint is to rub over it with a wax crayon in a contrasting tone to the walls. For example, a pale terracotta papered hall can look very good indeed with the woodwork rubbed over with green. To do an average long hallway would take approximately half an hour with two crayons.

FLOORS

Floors take the toughest beating of any surface in the house, so durability is as important as looks when it comes to choosing a covering. Every room has different requirements: hall and stairs need very hardwearing, non-slip flooring; in the kitchen it should be comfortable and practical; living rooms want comfort, good quality and appearance and the ability to withstand hard wear; bedrooms less so. You can economize on bedrooms but it would be foolish to do so in other rooms where you want the very best you can afford. Even if it eats up most of your budget it's still money well spent.

But before you spend anything, examine what you have in the way of flooring and see what can be done with it. Most wood, tile, vinyl and even old carpet can be cheered up somehow – cleaned, bleached, stained, painted, dyed, stencilled or covered with rugs.

ALL ABOUT STAINING

Floor stains have come a long way and are improving all the time. They are excellent for reviving tired old floors, modifying and improving the color and bringing out the wood grain. They are available in oil-, water- and alcohol-based mediums, and as each produces slightly different results each must be treated in a slightly different way.

The trickiest to use are the pigmented oil stains. They dry rather slowly and you must remember to wipe off excess when you use them, but they are worth the trouble because they do produce the most deeply even and gleaming results.

Dye stains come in concentrated form, soluble either in water or alcohol. The water-based mixtures go on easily and soak into the wood quickly,

Wooden fronts and panelling can hide a multitude of sins and used extensively impart a warm homey glow to a room. The effect can be varied by using different types of wood or stains as this converted attic shows so well. While the room to the right looks light, young and airy with lots of honey-toned panelling and simple furniture, the effect below is immediately more mature with a deeper stain, more traditional accessories and a splendid piano.

SANDING WOODEN FLOORS

Sanding machines can be rented, but you need to know how to use them. Ask for a drum sander which works with a belt of sandpaper revolving around a drum, and also for a hand-held sander for finishing off. Before you start you'll have to clear the room or cover everything up and go over the floor to remove nails. Wear dust mask and goggles and allow a day to prepare and a day to sand.

If you are working on a standard strip floor you will need two grades of sandpaper – medium and fine. If the surface is really bad, ask for a coarser grade. Start with the coarsest grade of paper and begin at one end of the room so that you can sand with the grain of the wood. On parquet use a medium grade and work diagonally. Start slowly. Tilt the machine back toward you so that the drum is on the floor, turn it on and slowly lower the machine. As soon as it touches the floor allow it to pull you forward, but not too fast. It needs controlling, but keep it moving at all costs or the sander will eat away at one particular place, making the floor uneven.

When you have finished one length of the room, tilt the machine so that the drum is raised again and drag it back across the room to where you started.

Position it so that the drum overlaps your first strip by around 3 inches, lower the machine and start again. Repeat this, changing the sandpaper when necessary (remembering to switch off the machine first). Use the rotary sander to cover all the parts the big machine misses. You will have to do corners and difficult edges by hand.

When you've done the whole floor, damp mop it, change the sandpaper to a finer grade and start at the other end of the room so that this time you are sanding in the opposite direction but with the grain. Repeat as before. Vacuum, then mop with a mixture of one part cider vinegar to four parts water; allow floor to dry completely.

At this stage you can either apply a protective couple of layers of polyurethane, letting each coat dry for at least 24 hours before applying the next, or you can stain or paint it. On a newly sanded floor you should first put down a sealer solution of half polyurethane and half mineral spirits, followed by coats of 100 percent polyurethane. Apply with a roller, and brush out any air bubbles. After a couple of days have passed and the sealing coat is thoroughly dry, apply two coats of wax and buff each coat with an electric floor polisher.

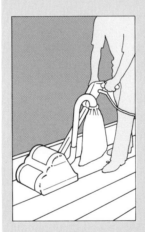

Rent a large floor sander and keep as straight and steady as possible to avoid scuffs and grooves.

A smaller hand-held sander will be required to reach into corners and to sand close to the baseboard.

Sweep up the worst of the dust then vacuum thoroughly several times to remove every trace.

Apply your chosen stain and varnish, allowing it to dry completely between coats for a fine finish.

but tend to dry in splotches. The alcohol-based varieties dry in an instant but if they spill over onto an already dry area you will get a build-up of color and an uneven look. Because the oil stain dries so much more slowly you have more control over the depth of tone. But before you darken the floor too much, remember that the protective coat of polyurethane will darken it still further. Remember too, that different woods will take stains in different ways so it's wise to test a little of the stain you want to use in a remote corner of the room before you go ahead and stain the whole floor. It is better to be safe now than sorry later when it is too late.

Most of these stains are available in bright colors as well as the conventional wood colors and you can mix concentrates together for more subtle shades and even use a fabric dye in a weaker strength than for clothes.

You can get some very glamorous effects with staining: alternating floorboards in different colors, for example; a dual- or three-toned pattern on parquet; a geometric pattern or motif drawn on the floor and colored in. If you do this you must lightly score around the edges of the design so that the stain does not leak or seep into the surrounding wood and spoil the effect.

Patience and ingenuity can be worth far more than unlimited funds when it comes to designing a room with flair and originality and this pleasant sunny rooms beats any expensive over-coordinated scheme hands down for interest and personality. Few of us can afford to redecorate and refurnish a room completely in one go; items have to be acquired gradually and blended with pieces we already have to create a look we like. It takes skill to blend family donated furniture, junk shop purchases and, possibly, a couple of brand new items, but how much more satisfying it is ultimately than the ubiquitous and often so dull matching sofa and chairs.

It is worth exercising your talents on the decorative effects too. A little paint goes a long way for relatively little cost with murals, stencils and special effects such as this homemade floor cloth. Don't be afraid to mix and match; experiment with colors and textures. Here, a fairly neutral gray and white background scheme becomes the unexpected but perfect foil for a collection of soft pastel colors and a random selection of inexpensive cane and wicker-work furniture from a variety of periods. The final effect is light, airy and spacious.

An inexpensive and ingenious idea borrowed from the 18th and 19th centuries, varnished floorcloths will provide you with a surprisingly hard-wearing rug effect at a fraction of the cost of the real thing. A piece of treated canvas is simply cut to a required size, the background color painted with a water-based interior paint and your proposed design marked out in chalk. Decorate using acrylic artists' paints and give a couple of coats of polyurethane varnish before turning back and gluing a narrow hem.

Dining chairs need not match to look good as a set. Here a collection of cane chairs have been painted in pastel colors to match the room and are related in texture and theme – if not in size and shape. Similarly, any odd chairs can look good together if stripped and varnished or painted to match.

A cheap garden table has been cleverly disguised for indoor use with a couple of pretty cloths. It not only makes a practical place to enjoy breakfast or a light meal with friends, but creates an attractive corner to place a vase of flowers and a few favorite objects.

An empty grate tends to look cold and bare if the fireplace is not in use. This one has been filled with a blaze of dried flowers, but fresh flowers, a spreading plant or a couple of leafy branches would look equally good.

Bare boards, stripped and stained gray, have been given a stencilled detail before varnishing. A border of flowers in pastel pink and green follows the line of the baseboard right around the room and provides a matching edging for the painted floorcloth (see below left) which was painted using matching colors. The same stencil could have been used equally effectively on walls, furniture and woodwork.

Plain glass shelves fitted into the chimney breast make good use of the space without being too obtrusive in a room which needs to make the most of all the space it has available.

This traditional style, real brick floor looks wonderful in a large, old fashioned kitchen, complete with wooden beams and large dining area. It is extremely hardwearing if not very comfortable underfoot and is particularly suitable for rooms such as this which open directly onto the garden and can be easily swept or mopped over when needed. A regular application of sealant prevents grease and dirt from building up.

BLEACHED FLOORS

Bleached wood floors look wonderful. They will also make a space seem larger. It is a long process but reasonably easy and inexpensive, and well worth the trouble. If the floor will take it (test a small out-of-the-way corner first), you can use ordinary household bleach. Scrub it well in and let it work away on the wood for 15 minutes or so. If it needs to be lighter, go on repeating the process until you like what you see. At this stage rinse the floor well with water and a mop, then finish off with a half-and-half solution of vinegar and water, which itself must be rinsed off with clear water.

All this neutralizing might well raise the grain of the wood again; if so, go over it lightly with sandpaper, then with vacuum cleaner and a damp mop before applying at least two coats of polyurethane with the statutory 24-hour wait between each one.

If household bleach doesn't seem to work, try the industrial strength. This achieves a really sun-bleached blond effect, but it is dangerous caustic stuff and you must follow the package directions explicitly. When using any bleach, wear rubber gloves and keep windows open.

LIGHTENING EFFECTS

You can also lighten a floor with white paint which you then wipe off almost immediately leaving a slight residue of film and little pockets here and there in small gaps, cracks and uneven areas. This film is then sealed by several layers of polyurethane and the result is pleasantly 'antiquated' and particularly good for a softwood such as pine.

It works just as well with creamy-white or ivory or a pearl gray paint and it is best to concentrate on one manageable area at a time rather than attempt the whole floor. Brush the paint on and after a few minutes wipe it off with a clean, dry cloth, working against the grain. Allow the floor to dry completely overnight before attempting to apply the sealing coats.

PAINTED FLOORS

If floors are too thin and worn to sand, or in an otherwise really bad state, you can probably still rescue them with paint. Or you can cover them with sheets of hardboard, and paint that. Do the same with old linoleum and composition tiled floors. You can simply brush on deck or yacht paint, or use a couple of coats of semigloss with protective coats of

It's not what you lay but the way you lay it: mock marble tiles in easy-care vinyl (far left) create a classic look for a large, elegant hallway, yet are far more practical and warm underfoot than the real thing. Simple wooden blocks (left) can look quite spectacular when laid like this. Contrasting wood shades have been arranged to form a stunning zigzag contained within a border. It gives an intricately patterned effect without using carpet and is quite simple to lay yourself, provided you work the pattern out first on graph paper.

polyurethane. More ambitiously, you can paint the floor then stencil a border on top, or brush on a variation of a wall-type glaze (see page 58) or try other techniques like marbling, or combing (dragging a coarse comb through the paint). Whether painting or staining, always finish off with polyurethane sealer. This can be reapplied every year or so for maximum protection. The only maintenance that your floor will need from now on is just a good thorough sweeping once a day and a light damp once-over with a mop.

CARPET OLD AND NEW

If carpet is too far gone it is better to take it up and try to do something with the floor underneath. If it's merely shabby or in a color or design you don't like, see if you can dye it. You might be warned off this – dye can spoil the quality – but if you hate it anyway you've nothing to lose. You can also cover a shabby plain carpet with rugs. You might be lucky enough to buy these in sales, or secondhand from junk shops, rummage or garage sales. Other reasonable alternatives are remnants, which make good area rugs; ask at a carpet store about these or, if you are near a carpet factory, enquire there. Finally, consider quilts from moving companies. These are those nicely stitched and ribbed 'rugs' that the more careful moving people use in their vans to cushion and protect furniture in transit. They come in interesting colors and the effect they create when on your floor can be absolutely stunning.

BUYING NEW

If you are determined and have budgeted to buy new carpet buy the best you can afford. Save and scrimp on other things, never on carpet. By the best I mean 80 percent wool/20 percent nylon, which will give you both quality and durability. However, there are some impressive synthetic fiber carpets now on the market which are specially dirt-resistant. They would be especially suitable for bedrooms, which undergo the least wear.

Look carefully at carpet labels to see what they're made of. If you want carpeting in your bathroom you should avoid wool; choose nylon, preferably rubber backed, which will dry fairly quickly after spills. You will find comfortable and attractive carpet which is made especially to be used in bathrooms. It is available in different textures and a whole range of widely fashionable colors.

This elegant hallway has cleverly avoided any gloomy corridor effect by making the most of a fine archway. Decoration is kept relatively simple to show off its fine proportions and large prints deliberately chosen for their recurring arched theme.

Natural burlap on the walls is not only a good neutral background for some fine traditional and natural features, it offers pattern and texture and a good hardwearing wallcovering in a heavy wear area.

The floor is a traditional English hallway design adapted to modern, easy-care materials. Stunning white marble tiles with inset black corners are in fact hardwearing vinyl tiles applied the same way: a lot softer underfoot and easier to wipe clean.

Don't forget to accessorize the hallway as you would any other room. Here a pair of handsome antique chairs and a smart leather umbrella stand satisfy both aesthetic and practical purposes.

A touch of the unexpected can always be relied on to lift a hallway out of the realms of the ordinary into something a little special. Here large terracotta urns have been filled with forced daffodil bulbs for early spring. Later in the year they will be replaced by hydrangea, marguerites and arrangements of autumn branches.

Lighting is unobtrusive but more than adequate: recessed downlights evenly spaced along the hallway with a brighter spotlight over the front door.

Halls are never easy to decorate for, by their very nature, they present a special range of problems. Basically, they either seem too small to serve any particularly useful purpose or they are simply large, featureless corridors with doors. Many people when faced with a difficult hall, are daunted by the challenge and respond by treating the threatening area as something to be quickly painted and forgotten. Yet with just a little flair and imagination you can create a really welcoming entrance to your home – and you may even be able to turn the space to some useful advantage as well.

If, for example, you are short of space you may be able to slip in a small desk or even a shower or walk-in closet under the stairs. It is a wise rule always to consider every corner as a potential mini 'room'. Explore the possibilities of folding tables and chairs, tiny-size basins and other space-savers.

Decoration, too, needs careful consideration. First and foremost, floors should be hardwearing because this is an area with a lot of heavy traffic: consider top-grade carpet or heavy-duty vinyl flooring which is easy to clean; tough burlap or vinyl papers on the walls. Lighting needs some thought too. A dark, dingy hallway is not only depressing, it can also be dangerous for both the young and the elderly. Bright spotlights bounced off walls or ceiling, or recessed downlights all provide good, bright light without dazzling the eyes. A dimmer switch is also a useful option.

This small hall has been given a life and character of its own with clever use of color and accessories. Inexpensive, plain vinyl tiles have been laid imaginatively, following the hall around the corner with a wide border of charcoal gray against a gray/white marbled effect. A random yellow tile has triggered off a recurring theme: yellow painted door frame, picture frame and modern coat-rack. A simple plant stand has been given a new lease on life with black, yellow and turquoise gloss paints and simple bracket shelving used to create a mini 'office'. The chair can be folded and put out of the way when not in use.

MADE FOR HARD WEAR

Carpet tiles are a good idea in overworked areas like halls and children's rooms or if you live in a rented place or move often. They can be moved around, easily taken up, replaced and come in quite good colors. Sisal carpeting is pretty tough too – and feels it if you are barefoot. But it is reasonably priced, looks neat and nicely textured. It also goes well with many different styles of furniture; and looks just as effective when used in an urban apartment as it is in a country house setting.

MATTING

It used to be cheap; it isn't any more. But it looks terrific with any style of furnishing and is also very chic. It is now available in all sorts of handsome twists and weaves and herringbones from fine to coarse and from pale sand colors to much darker mixtures. It is not advisable for stairs because it is inclined to be slippery; children and elderly people would find it dangerous. It needs to be vacuumed like a carpet or, better still, given an occasional sweep with a stiff broom to get the dust out. Stains can be scrubbed out with a brush, or if hard to get out, removed with carpet cleaner.

TILES

Good composition tiles lend themselves to all sorts of handsome designs. Plain vinyls look good and wear well and you can relieve any monotony with a contrasting border. Rubber tiles are comfortable underfoot and perfect for a chic, high-tech room. The timeless beauty of durable ceramic tiles is ideal for any room where cost, comfort, and warmth are less important than looks. Sealed cork tiles are not only warm, but also practical and attractive. What may enhance their appeal even more is that they are easy to lay yourself.

Ceramic tiles make an attractive, extremely hardwearing floor surface for rooms such as kitchens and bathrooms which are prone to spills and splashes. Here, plain white, floor-quality tiles have been interspersed with a harlequin random pattern effect using plain colored tiles from the same line.

WINDOWS

First of all, close your eyes to the fact that elaborate curtains in all their Victorian splendor and theatricality are right back in fashion, lavish with ruffles, ruches, swags, bows and handsome headings. This sort of elegance costs a lot of money.

You can still have beautiful or interesting windows without expensive curtains. If you have a view, make the most of it and leave the windows uncovered. Enhance the view by painting the outside woodwork to act as a frame; use a strong vibrant color which will make the window into a very positive feature. If you prefer privacy, attach split bamboo or matchstick blinds spray-painted the same bright color. Paint them a deep color, and they will filter sunlight through into the room in a very interesting way. Paper shades look surprisingly

If you are lucky enough to inherit a fine set of window shutters it is generally worth stripping them back and re-staining and varnishing. Check that they are in good condition and free of termites before you start. This graceful window has the added bonus of some fine panelling which has also been finished to match the frame, shutters and baseboard.

It is comparatively easy to alter visually the size or shape of a window, particularly in the kitchen where curtains aren't always the most practical alternative. Here a sturdy shelf across its width displays an interesting collection of kitchen paraphernalia, while utensils hang ready at hand below. Because most of the items are glass or wire mesh, they distract the eye from concentrating on both the over-long frame and the dull view, without blocking too much light from the window.

good and it is worth considering how little they cost. Finally, while they won't last for years, they're quite tough and durable.

If your house has inside shutters, they're worth keeping, both as protection against drafts and for extra security. Paint them all over or pick out panels. Louvered shutters have a less heavy appearance and again fill the room with soft filtered light. In comparison, they will cost less than good curtains and take up less space.

Window shades are excellent and come in a good range of colors, sizes and fabrics. Even if your windows are not stock size it is quite easy to trim these shades down. Plain ones can be painted or decorated with a thin border as long as it doesn't impede the action of the roller. Or make your own window shades. If you have stock size windows, it might even be possible to buy ready-made decorator-effect window coverings, such as festoon or Roman shades.

Turn your window into a miniature conservatory by fitting it with glass or wooden shelves and filling them with plants and flowers. Or use it to house a collection of colored glassware. Or simply hang plants from hooks in front of the window or from poles stretched across it, and you will have turned an annoying problem spot and potential eyesore into a focal point and beautiful niche.

Transform small windows completely by making

them into slender French windows. Buy two lengths of 2 by 4 inch lumber, pre-cut to your floor-to-ceiling height, and secure them on either side of the window frame. Paint them in with the walls or in a contrasting color or cover them with fabric. Fill in with full-length sheer or muslin curtains or a long plain blind and you will have, in effect, a very graceful window indeed.

CURTAINS WITH A DIFFERENCE

If you're set on fabric at the window, copy a sumptuous stately home idea and have decorative valances and draped swags of material or, a simpler version, a single piece of fabric draped across a pole. This looks magnificent and costs a fraction of a proper curtain's price. You can compromise too by having one length of fabric instead of the usual two; loop it back to one side during the day to allow light into the room; let it drop at night to screen the room from view and give you complete privacy – simply and elegantly.

If you don't need to draw the curtains across at night you can get away with shams, using less material and letting them hang flat, not gathered in any way, at each side. A good quality remnant would be ideal for this.

Economizing on curtains never means skimping. Masses of cheap fabric like sheer nylon, plain cotton, muslin, even curtain lining, that looks full and generous, is far better than a spartan amount of costly stuff. And don't forget that attractive bedspreads, tablecloths, and even sheets can all be made into very acceptable curtains and do very well as temporary measures while you are saving up for something better. Indeed sheeting can be painted with fabric dye to match your furnishings.

Poles needn't be expensive, either; plastic tubing, wooden dowels or poles from a hardware or home improvement store, even broom handles and drain pipes can be made to look good. Have them cut to fit, then stain or paint them. Finish them off with door knobs on the ends.

This theatrical dining room could afford a dramatic window treatment. Roman shades add an exotic splash of pattern, picking up the gray and raspberry of walls and woodwork. To heighten the effect, a raspberry striped fabric has been simply hemmed and draped over a gray-painted wood pole running the length of both windows to provide instant valance and dress curtains using a minimum of fabric.

Conservatory screen

Tab-headed café curtain

Austrian blind

Single-draped window

WINDOW DRESSING

There are many ways you can dress a window depending on what effect you are trying to achieve. Here a plain, twelve-pane window changes its image according to its treatment. A tab-headed café curtain on a simple pole or a series of shelves with a screen of green plants look smart and practical; a flouncy Austrian blind makes it look longer and very pretty; a single draped curtain adds width.

/// While it's essential and wise to spend money first on getting the basics – floors, walls, ceilings, windows and lighting – in good shape, this probably leaves very little for furnishing. It could be a blessing in disguise. The more money you have, the more likely you are to rush out and buy something you might regret later. If you're aiming at a truly individual room and not an instant package, it's best to let it evolve slowly. Tastes as well as finances change over the years, usually for the better, so leave room to accommodate them.

MAKE A LIST

As usual the first sensible thing to do when planning the furniture is to make a list of any existing pieces you might have and decide whether it's worth spending money having them upholstered, re-covered, refinished or repainted. Then you can progress to a list of all the other pieces that you would like, in order of priority, and what they are likely to cost. Spend time window-shopping and keeping tabs on prices in sales, advertisements and so on. Make a note of what you can actually afford now and what to save for – how much and for how long.

NEW VERSUS OLD

There are three types of furniture which will cost a great deal of money: anything brand new, modern classics and genuine antiques. So forget them for the time being. Think instead about what can possibly be improvised, made yourself or rehabilitated. Junk shop pieces with potential and good secondhand furniture are better than new stuff which is shoddy and which will not last and will look shabby in no time.

Having said that, there are major exceptions. Beds, for instance. Never stint on beds. Buy the best you can afford and even if you build the base or platform yourself, the mattress should be of the best quality you can get.

A good quality bed should top your list of essentials. This stylish futon combines the advantages of reasonable comfort with an affordable price and needs a minimum of accessories to look good: simple woodblock flooring, a plain chest of drawers, mirror and a wooden screen.

Study areas often have to be squeezed into a corner of the bedroom. Here a good run of worktop surface and storage fits perfectly into the design of this bedroom with space to sit and relax or watch TV in the bargain. Blue, white and yellow has been chosen as the main color scheme, bright and businesslike for study.

With space at a premium in this multipurpose room, the work area has been built around the window to make the most of the natural light. The alcoves have been screened from view, which has created instant wardrobe storage.

With the bed centrally placed in the room, a three-tier cart makes a highly functional bedside valet to be wheeled into service when and where needed. Desk area doubles as dressing table when required; bright yellow filing cabinets store documents and clothes.

A simple painted white length of plywood resting on a few brightly colored filing cabinets intended for office use makes an excellent wall-to-wall work area with shelves above. A folding chair is a good choice if you are short of space.

Plain white fabric window shades have been fitted to screen recesses on either side of the chimney breast to provide a hidden closet area without the expense of fitted doors or units. Blind at the window has been chosen to match.

Plain blue felt stretched and stapled over the chimney breast makes an interesting feature of it and matches the deep blue carpet. A flat screen TV has been set into the wall to save valuable floor space.

Conventional positioning of furniture doesn't always make best use of space, particularly when the room serves more than one purpose. Here the bed has been placed centrally, back to back with a sofa: unexpected but it works. The back of the sofa makes a good padded headboard.

Even the cheapest shelving systems can work out to be expensive. Here homemade shelves have been fitted around the window and painted white to match the wall so that visually they take up very little space. Worktop over filing cabinets is equally inexpensive.

A cart is always useful for providing flexible storage facilities. This smart black one is good for book work as well as necessary clothes and toiletries.

Good light is essential for desk work. Here the window provides adequate natural light during the day and is supplemented by a couple of useful adjustable desk lamps which can double as bedside reading lamps at night.

Chairs that are going to be sat in for long periods at a desk or table should be well-designed, comfortable and support the back, but they needn't be bulky. These tubular chrome chairs take up minimum space visually, yet serve their purpose very well.

The same ruling applies to any big upholstered pieces like sofas and armchairs. It's rarely worth buying these secondhand; they usually need drastic, i.e. expensive, treatment. Don't worry, though; it all evens out. If you have to spend on decent, comfortable seating you can save by being clever about smaller items like coffee tables, end tables, work tables, dining and dressing tables and occasional chairs, all of which can be quite easily improvised. With almost any piece of upholstery, however – and this includes mattresses – the price reflects the quality. You get what you pay for. Since the quality is something you have to take on trust – you can't usually see the frames, filling and springs – your safest course is to go to a reputable dealer or store. Do ask questions, the salesperson will be glad to help.

In a one-room or small apartment, it might be best to consider a divan or sofa bed, which can always be used in a sitting room or study-cum-guest room later. Again, it should be the best you can afford for maximum comfort and staying power.

Where a room serves more than one purpose, choose furniture carefully to make the most of available space. Here a floor-length cloth makes a round dining table pretty enough to look good in a living room with cane easy chairs for both sitting and dining.

INSPIRATION AND IMPROVISATION

A round dining table (space saving and better for conversation) is easy enough to make yourself. Or have a basic one made very inexpensively by a local carpenter. Even a fairly battered one from a junk shop would do as long as it's steady. Cover it and all its imperfections with a permanent floor-length cloth and a series of coordinating overcloths. They're simple to make and a clean one each day would still be cheaper than the cost of a new table.

/ / / Small occasional tables made in the same way as the round dining table are useful for filling up corners and as coffee tables.

/ / / Sheets of glass cut to your specification, with rounded or squared-off edges, can be placed on all sorts of bases, such as plant pots, bricks, wooden blocks, to make perfectly satisfactory coffee tables. Ensure that any base is strong and stable enough so the table will be secure and that the edges are smoothed and corners are rounded.

/ / / Basic plywood cubes are simple to make and come in handy all over the house. Painted, lacquered, stained, or mirrored, they will serve as small side tables; covered with a layer of foam rubber, then with carpet or upholstery fabric, they make good stools, with or without castors.

/ / / Perfectly good study desks or tables can be made with hollow core flush doors (easily obtained from lumberyards or home improvement centers for very little money) or any other old door with a flat surface. Give them a smart finish with paint, lacquer or stain and set them on painted or natural wooden trestles, or sawhorses, or 2 by 2 steel supports. Consider using file cabinets which are not only a good base, but quite a practical one.

/ / / Dressing tables and dressing tables-cum-desks for bedrooms that also have to act as home offices can be made by painting or lacquering unfinished wood chests. Set them a kneehole's width apart against a wall and top them with a length of wood, laminated with plastic, about 1-1½ inches thick. This sort of practical, easy-to-clean and maintain top could be used over a run of painted filing cabinets and not look out of place. In fact, it will look custom-made and very special.

/ / / Bed bases can be dispensed with and a small room made to look bigger by topping a carpet-covered platform with a well-covered mattress. A platform like this has the advantage of appearing to divide up a space without actually taking up any extra room. The platform itself can be designed to open up for storage.

This handsome double bed platform, not only makes an effective room divider but also serves as a comfortable sitting and lounging area during the day with the addition of rugs, pillows and bolster cushions – even a bowl of flowers.

An awkward sloping roof in an attic bedroom has been cleverly utilized by building a stepped seating unit into the space and continuing the carpet up over it. It makes an inviting and unusual window seat.

/ / / If you are handy, or you can get the job done reasonably by a local carpenter, build a platform at one end of the room to take the place of conventional sofas and armchairs. Use plywood or hollow core doors and cover the platform with carpet and piles of floor cushions or pillows. Or make a seating pit by boxing in a chosen area. Carpet both levels and fill the center with floor cushions and a coffee table. Another way is to build a surrounding platform higher and slightly further back and add a second carpeted level at seating height.

/ / / If you have to find room for both storage and seating in a small space here's how to get two for the price of one. Build in boxes all around the room, or along one side, or under a window. Give them hinged lids for storage and add thick slabs of foam rubber covered with fabric for seating. Suspend fabric-covered foam rubber slabs from a brass or wood pole secured to the wall at the back, for good back support and to add a handsome look.

/ / / Make window seats wherever possible to provide inconspicuous and inexpensive extra seating and storage. If your windows don't lend themselves to such treatment build a frame around them and slip a window seat across.

/ / / Use lidded wicker laundry baskets or even tin trunks as bedside tables or side tables.

FOUND FURNITURE

Scrounge around secondhand, thrift and junk shops for bargains and keep an eye open for discards near trash bins. Scrutinize even the most unpromising looking hand-me-downs and castoffs. As long as the shape is reasonable, almost any piece can be revamped and spruced up beyond recognition by stripping off old paint, varnish and dirt and painting or lacquering or just repolishing the newly cleaned surface.

Old mismatched kitchen chairs can look stunning if they are stripped and painted, each one a different primary color, or given a harlequin effect with, say, a basically white finish and different colored legs or backs. Or they can be painted plain white and given smart printed cushions or pads. This will pull together an assortment of different sized chairs and make it look as though they match. You can obtain the same effect by painting the chairs all the same color.

Dull mass-produced chairs can be given a totally new look with either plain paint or a marbled or dragged finish; old chests of drawers or dressers can be stripped, sanded and waxed or painted and stencilled. Old cane furniture can be spray painted in any color that is suitable to the decor of a particular room.

What you're looking for is *potential*. You may not be able to use or fit in a particular piece of furniture as it stands but could you use part of it? Visualize it with the legs chopped off, the size reduced, the mirror removed, the ornamentation gotten rid of. Is there perhaps another smaller, plainer piece of furniture inside it waiting to get out? Would that huge cupboard divide into two? Learn not to dismiss anything out of hand if it's in good condition; go back and give it a long hard appraisal. You *can* make a silk purse out of a sow's ear. The sort of place where you might pick up promising items is limited only by your imagination – or by sheer luck. On pages 86-87 we detail a few of the most likely sources of secondhand and castoff furniture.

Even a simple bed can be transformed into something special with the right accessories. Built into a bedside complex (above) and given a vibrant patchwork bed cover, it is very much an integral part of this dramatic black and white room. The romantic bedroom (left) was created by adding a brass rail headboard and draped curtains.

Combined living/dining rooms in newer houses are often a good size and well-proportioned but somewhat lacking in character. This fine combination room had the advantages of a large square arch effect between the two areas and generous patio doors at the dining room end, visually extending the space and providing plenty of light.

Natural fiber flooring and apricot rag-rolled effect wallpaper immediately added a warm glow and dissipated some of the 'newness'; this was coordinated with cream for softness and accented with powder blue. The scheme was kept deliberately simple to accentuate the feeling of space and light with a fine, square-cut cream sofa and plain cream blinds at the windows. Built-in shelves and cabinets, neater, more streamlined and less expensive than freestanding units, were built around the patio doors to provide storage for china, books and items on display. It provides the perfect backdrop for a large circular dining table, draped with an apricot rag-roll effect cloth to match the paper and topped with a shorter blue cloth to match the seat covers on a set of rattan dining chairs. By day, when the room is not in use for eating, the draped table and attractive, comfortable armchairs effectively become an extension of the living room, a pleasant place to sit and read, open mail or whatever, especially since the tablecoths have been coordinated with cushions on the sofa to provide a visual link between the two areas.

Large floorstanding tubs and baskets filled with houseplants are strategically placed throughout, not only to add touches of fresh greenery, but also to blend with the tubs of plants on the patio outside and thus draw the eye outside, making the room seem even larger than it is.

The uneven, mottled effect of rag-rolling adds interest to a large expanse of plain wall without being as overpowering as a pattern. A mock, rag-roll effect paper has been used here.

Sisal flooring is tough, hardwearing and inexpensive for large areas and particularly suited to rooms which open onto the garden, or homes with pets.

Large chunky sofa in cream makes a good visual room divider and matches the blinds and woodwork. This one has the added bonus that it converts easily into a double bed for short-stay guests.

Built-in shelves and cabinets are economical on space and money. These run from floor to ceiling to provide much needed storage for china and cutlery and have been used to frame the large patio windows.

Floor-length cloths, chosen to match the overall color scheme of the two rooms, disguise a less than perfect dining table and make it more suited to daytime use.

Simple cream shades, edged in apricot, enhance the feeling of light and space. Drapes would have created a rather fussier, more formal effect.

Recessed ceiling lights are much neater, subtler and more effective than a single pendant light and they can be positioned where they are needed.

Ice-cream colors blend well in both living and dining areas and are a good, soft accompaniment to the natural finish of the sisal matting and rattan chairs.

A simple window seat built into a bay window not only provides a pleasant place to sit, but, properly integrated and coordinated with the rest of the room, turns it into a special feature and makes the room look larger.

If you have a conventional or gas fireplace, try to include a selection of shiny surfaces nearby, such as polished cast iron, brass and glass to catch the flickering firelight.

A small table that has seen better days, or an inexpensive particleboard model can be transformed by a couple of long cloths to match your other upholstery fabrics. Alternatively, if the table is sturdy, rag-roll to match the walls.

Don't be afraid to mix old and new and different styles of furniture. You will find that antiques often blend surprisingly well with more modern pieces.

Color blending need not be difficult once you have chosen the basis for your general design. The scheme for this room was developed from the pastel check fabric used to cover the window seat. A soft apricot was selected for the wallpaper and other colors chosen for cloths and cushions: peaches, blues and greens. Patterned fabric is often more expensive than plain; so here a minimum amount of pattern is used to maximum effect by boosting with solid-color fabrics.

If you don't want to or can't use curtains at the window but feel window shades are a little too plain, pleated Roman shades might well be the answer. Many made-to-order services include them in their line these days – or make your own. Equally effective but rather softer and fussier are Austrian blinds, or balloon shades, which gather the fabric in a series of flounced ruches.

Both elements of this dual-purpose room work well together. The larger part of the room is the living area which continues the apricot and cream theme and fresh ice-cream colors for a warm relaxing atmosphere. Rag-roll effect wallpaper and sisal flooring run straight through from the dining room to the living room area which gives a feeling of continuity and also helps link these two special-purpose areas visually.

A fine bay window at the extreme end has been made into a special feature by covering the wide sill in a padded foam cushion to create a comfortable window seat. Upholstered in a fine pastel check fabric and plumped full of piped cushions picking out the apricot, blue and green checks, it is both useful and attractive. Cream Roman shades with matching apricot trim down the sides and along the hem really set off the window to best advantage – and they capitalize on the colors of the room itself. They also take up less room and light than drapes used in the same position.

The true focal point of the room is a handsome fireplace with a waxed pine mantelpiece and marble surround which is light and elegant to suit the rest of the scheme. A traditional firebasket supports a gas fire that produces a warm, welcoming flame that is controlled from an inconspicuous handle – all the appeal of traditional fuel without the work or dirt.

A good-looking cream wool rug lightens the floor area, the perfect partner for the cream detailed sofa, with its mass of appliqued and plain throw pillows and cloths, all in coordinating colors:– apricots, creams and blues.

Remember textures as well as color when planning the design of a room, especially when using plain papers and fabrics. Note how the relief effect of rug and sofa contrasts with the gleam of marble and silky cushions.

Large, leafy plants will add not only life and color to a room, but interesting shapes and shadows too. Stand them in large tubs or baskets, or even pots and containers which are intended to be used in the garden.

At night, with the lights dimmed over the living area and the recessed lights spotlighting the dining table, attention is focused on the other end of the room. A full-length cream window shade shuts out the night, but it can be raised on finer evenings, to great effect, revealing the spotlit patio. Apricot candles and cream napkins coordinate the blue tablecloth perfectly with the rest of the room; the table is laid with the best china and crystal to catch the flickering firelight from the next room. A door opening directly to the kitchen offers easy access for the busy cook or hostess.

ANTIQUE SHOPS Don't be put off, even if they look rather grand. It is quite often possible to find bargains in shops that specialize in a particular period but have had to buy most of an estate to get certain treasures. The rest of the contents are often sold off at half their real value so it is worth paying regular visits to shops in your neighborhood. Poke around in the back of the shop – that's where the 'finds' will be. You never know what you'll stumble across, and it's an enjoyable way to develop an eye for beautiful things.

Attractive tie-on covers will transform the dingiest chair (right) and they are far simpler and cheaper than a complete reupholstery job – and far easier to replace and keep clean.

CLASSIFIED ADVERTISEMENTS OR NOTICES IN SUPER-MARKETS It is always a sensible idea to read through newspaper advertisement columns of items for sale. Notice boards in supermarkets will tell you not only about things for sale but about forthcoming rummage and church sales, and possibly garage, estate and liquidation sales.

SECONDHAND AND JUNK SHOPS Always worth browsing around because their stock turns over frequently. Some buy up whole estates and you can take your pick; others simply sell old but not antique furniture plus the odd wonderful find that has crept in by accident. There are nearly always nice bits of glass, china, fabric and maybe picture frames and other odds and ends for which you might have a use.

FLEA MARKETS AND STREET MARKETS There are two kinds: the permanent variety where the pickings have almost certainly been gone over first by other dealers; and the transients who set up their

stalls and then move on somewhere else the next day. Either way you could be lucky, especially if you can get there early.

STREETS Always look near dumpsters outside houses that are being renovated, especially in well-heeled areas. I have seen marble fireplaces, bathtubs and basins in first-class condition and really nice old doors and panelling – all thrown out. Sometimes you even find pieces of good furniture. If you're interested in any item, ask at the door –

don't just take it; more often than not the owners will be glad to let you have it for free.

THRIFT AND CHARITY STORES Some of these shops sell furniture and small household items for private owners on a commission basis; others sell goods given to help a charity.

MOVING AND STORAGE COMPANIES Some companies hold annual sales of unclaimed goods, which can yield terrific bargains although you do have to be prepared to wait while dozens of packing cases are dealt with before you get to anything decent. Call companies up when you know about them, or look them up in the Yellow Pages and ask if they hold such sales.

AUCTIONS You will find details of forthcoming furniture auctions in local papers. Even if you think you won't be able to afford anything, it's still worth going to have a look around and to sit in for a while to get some idea of prices.

DEMOLITION AND WRECKING COMPANIES Any building that is torn down generally results in a hoard of architectural details like staircases, fireplaces, cornices, and moldings, not to mention furniture, even flooring. This is especially true of old theaters and movie theaters, hotels, churches, and office buildings. Keep an eye open for notices of such sales, or call up a relevant company if you see its notice on a building.

SECONDHAND OFFICE FURNITURE SHOPS Here you might find a cache of old chairs, tables, desks, filing cabinets or shelving with good potential, that are often sold off very cheaply.

RESTAURANT, SCHOOL AND HOSPITAL SUPPLIERS These are excellent sources for carts, commercial stoves, gym lockers (good for storage), strong wire or metal shelving, cabinets, cheap tables and chairs.

GARAGE AND TAG SALES The bargains that these sales yield are legendary. Prices are usually negotiable.

Keep your eye open for interesting and attractive items that can be put to new use. This superb brassbound chest (left) was repaired and restained before finally being stencilled. The result is a most acceptable and attractive table for the living room. What had been a cast-off piece of furniture with no future and destined for scrap has now been transformed into the stylish focal point of this split-level, simply decorated living/dining room. A real bonus is the additional storage space which it provides.

This formerly plain wooden chest and mirror frame were given a highly individual touch with stencilling to match the floor and the dado stencils in the room where they were placed. A thin green line has been added to the chest to add extra definition.

WHAT TO LOOK FOR

Before you buy any item of furniture, however much a bargain it is, make sure that it will actually work well for you. Will it go through your door and up your stairs or in your elevator? Do the drawers work? Do the chairs and tables wobble? Does it have dry rot? Is it too far gone to repair? Is there termite damage? Is the piece badly weathered? Is the veneer lifting up? Look at everything very carefully and always take a tape measure and your room plan with you on shopping expeditions. Choose shapes that are simple and well proportioned. Don't be put off by details that can be easily changed: hideous handles and knobs, for instance. In fact, renewing elements like these will give you an opportunity to put your own stamp on a piece of furniture.

WHEN TO PAINT AND HOW

Some pieces of old furniture will only need thorough cleaning or stripping. The most important thing in this case is to take off the old finish and get down to clean wood that can be stained or oiled and waxed.

Obviously really fine wood or wood with a beautiful natural grain should only be treated in this way. Quality items deserve quality care.

Otherwise, painting is usually the answer for pieces of furniture that have been repaired, those made of ugly wood and fairly new but undistinguished pieces that are nevertheless in reasonable shape.

Painted furniture, of course, has a fine pedigree. There is almost no civilization or period that has not produced interesting examples, and alongside these sophisticated pieces there has grown up a tradition

*Sometimes stripping,
varnishing and a new set
of handles is all that is
needed – like this
handsome old chest of
drawers now restored to
former glory.*

*Cane and wicker
furniture takes paint well
– it is usually quicker to
spray – and can be
painted to match your
color scheme. Here an
old wicker chair, cane
table top and part of the
headboard have been
painted white just to set
off this beautiful
patchwork quilt.*

of folk and rustic painting, sensible as well as decorative. So your painted furniture will be in good company.

One of the simplest and most effective ways of painting furniture that has been cleaned and stripped is to apply a coat or two of oil-based flat wall paint. You can have any color you want if you tint the base coat with a stain or universal tinting color (available at specialist paint stores), or with artists' oil colors. When the top coat is *completely* dry, sand it all over with a fine grade sandpaper until it is quite smooth. Wipe the surface with a clean, dry cloth and then give the whole thing a coat or two of proper varnish (as opposed to polyurethane) which can either be matte, semigloss or gloss.

New wood (like unpainted wood) will first need a coat of primer, preferably the white oil-based primer which is sold especially for wood. It should be thinned down with paint thinner or turpentine – three parts primer to one part thinner – applied generously and worked well into the wood. If you are working on pine, any knots in the wood must first be sealed before priming, with a special knot sealer available from hardware stores. If you do not do this, the knots will go on oozing resin for years, and this will crack and discolor the paint making an unsightly mess that is awkward to deal with later.

If you have the time, the patience and the aptitude, there are dozens of different paint finishes of varying sophistication that can be applied. Most of the finishes previously recommended for walls can be used but it's wise to try them out first on a piece of primed board until you feel you're getting the desired effect.

COMPROMISING SITUATIONS

While it's sensible and practical to have a reasonably clear long-term view of how you want your rooms to look, it might be years before you're in a position to achieve your ambitions. In the meantime you have to live with what you've got, adding gradually what you can afford and always arranging the room so that it never looks incomplete. So it's fatal to be too rigid about what goes where; it should be as flexible as possible so that nothing is ever wasted. For example, a pair of inexpensive canvas or cane occasional chairs could start off life in the living room but end up in the bedroom or even as garden chairs; an old chest of drawers can be moved from the master bedroom to take on a new lease on life in a child's room, perhaps looking completely different with paint or stencils.

If you are really short of space in a small apartment or studio, you could keep a small occasional table by a window seat and add a larger folding top for dining. When you have proper dining space later, the fold-down top will still come in useful for parties and entertaining.

The main thing is not to be too set in your ideas. Compromising doesn't mean putting up with something you don't like but rather being a clever opportunist who can turn limited space and materials into something original and creative.

STRIPPING FURNITURE

You must know what a particular finish is before you can remove it properly. Sometimes this is difficult to determine so you should first rub it with paint thinner or denatured alcohol. If this does not work, try paint stripper.

Remove any old handles or hinges. Cover the surrounding area with old newspaper or plastic tarps, wear a pair of rubber gloves and a surgical mask or scarf over your mouth (in case of poisonous fumes), and apply the stripper with an old paintbrush, having first read the instructions on the can. The top layer will take about ten minutes to soften. When it is all bubbly, scrape the sticky-looking substance off large surfaces with a broad-bladed paint scraper, taking care not to mark the wood in any way. Clean up tricky surfaces with coarse and then fine grades of steel wool. Be patient, because it can take several applications of paint remover before you finally get down to the original surface of the wood.

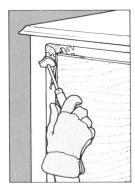

It is important to wear protective clothing when using any kind of chemical paint remover. Patch test and apply, following instructions carefully. A broad-blade paint **scraper will remove the worst of the dissolved paint; use a smaller, curved-blade scraper to deal with beadings and any detail and finish with coarse and then fine steel wool.**

If you can't afford a carpet and curtains at first, improvise with less expensive rugs and blinds (above). Furniture, too, can be improvised with a little ingenuity. This random selection is linked by shape and color, while old stripped chests (right) serve a multitude of purposes from seats and tables to storage.

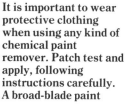

A beautiful bedroom needn't cost a fortune. Here coordinating fabrics and wallpaper have been used most effectively to create a romantic but sophisticated atmosphere. The double bed has been made into a handsome feature by creating a canopied half-tester effect from the ceiling with the headboard padded in matching fabric. If your bedroom is big enough you could even turn the bed into an old fashioned four poster with curtains at all four corners.

Walls are softly marbled using a mock marble paper, slightly more expensive but certainly quicker and easier to apply than attempting it yourself with paints, coordinated with a matching fabric and highlighted in pale blue. The overall effect is cool, calm and tranquil with fully adjustable wooden shutters to let in filtered light as and when needed. Other little touches of luxury which are easily copied and needn't be expensive are the bedside tables, cheap and cheerful but cleverly disguised beneath long cloths, an old but comfortable chair and lots of small color-coordinated cushions on the bed laid against ruffled pillow shams.

A simple wooden valance covered in gathered fabric and hung with lined curtains makes a very effective half tester.

If there is a lot going on in the rest of the room, keep windows simple. These shutters can be folded open or opened like a louvre.

Most houses these days are usually supplied with built-in closets that rarely conform to how you want your bedroom to look. Paint or paper can be used to effect a very simple disguise; here matching marble paper makes a run of floor-to-ceiling closets extremely sleek and smart, but they could just as easily have been painted or covered in fabric. The same tactics could be applied to built-in drawers and cabinets that have seen better days in an older property provided they are sound (check wood and hinges), or even to freestanding secondhand wardrobes. For equally successful transformations, try transfers or using stencilling.

Bedside lamps are essential and should be easily accessible from the bed. These swing out on a swivel arm for extra flexibility.

Small cushions can be made up inexpensively from fabric remnants in a wide range of shapes and colors to suit your decorating scheme.

A comfortable chair is always useful in the bedroom for dressing and undressing as well as just relaxing and reading.

Small inexpensive tables which you can make yourself or buy in plyboard make an ideal bedside surface when covered.

Wall-to-wall carpet makes sense in the bedroom and because it doesn't get a lot of wear can be chosen from less expensive lines.

KITCHENS & BATHROOMS

/// **V**ery few of us walk into our ideal kitchen or bathroom. Even if the fixtures are brand new and the space generous, it still might not coincide with our dream versions. So we all have to make do, at first, with what we buy or lease. Just as well, because this gives scope for our ideas – and those of manufacturers and designers – to evolve and it leaves room for improvements and new developments.

KITCHENS

If you are starting from scratch, you can plan carefully from the word go. Even if you can't afford the big appliances you would like at the outset you must allow for the space to accommodate them and also take them into account when you are having wiring and plumbing installed.

If you intend to stay in the house a long time or plan to extend your family, allow for as much storage and counter space as you can.

The kitchen you end up with depends to some extent on what sort of cook you are. A dedicated cook with a demanding job will need lots of food storage and quick cooking facilities, i.e., large refrigerator or freezer and a microwave oven. Single people and couples without children or those who are not very fond of cooking will still want an efficient kitchen, even if it's just for heating up and serving convenience food or leftover take-out food and producing ice and washing dishes. They might require less storage and different equipment – a refrigerator/freezer rather than a big separate free-standing freezer.

People who really enjoy cooking will need space for herbs, spices, cookbooks, special ingredients, gadgets and special equipment. Possessors of beautiful pans and dishes will probably want them to be on show or at hand, calling for the sort of storage that displays rather than hides – shelving instead of cabinets, for instance. And it's not just how good a cook you are that will be reflected in your kitchen, but what sort: neat, tidy, well organized, able to cook calmly in a shoebox, or chaotic, needing heaps of elbow room and surface space and every pan in the place.

Assuming you have the space you must decide whether you want to eat in the kitchen. Will it cope with family meals, full-scale entertainment or will an eating counter be enough?

Combining kitchen with dining room and/or pantry could give you the extra space you need. Here crisp white and gray with a touch of warm yellow adds to the feeling of light and space. Simple white table and fold-away chairs take up little room; storage is sleek and commodious.

///95

BASIC KITCHEN PLANS

The majority of kitchens fall into four standard shapes for planning: U-shaped, island, L-shaped and galley or corridor kitchen. Anything more awkward or unusual than this is usually adapted in some way to fit one of these shapes. U-shaped is probably the most popular form for the average size kitchen: a continuous run of cabinets along three sides of the room to create a flexible and easy-to-use working environment. Larger rooms are usually adapted to an island or peninsula layout to help break up a large expanse of floor area. Island units can be shaped according to the design of the room. Awkward L-shaped rooms need careful planning and clever use of cabinets to make best use of space; the smallest kitchen, the corridor or galley, works best if cabinets are run along one wall, providing a continuous work sequence in minimum space.

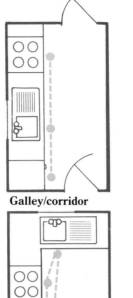
Galley/corridor

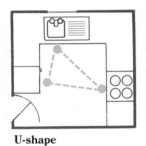
U-shape

Island

L-shape

MAKING DO

Most of us never get the chance to start from scratch. If we are moderately lucky we walk into a reasonable kitchen in any house we buy or rent and just have to fit in with it. All too often it's a mess, with a tangle of pipes, unsightly and inadequate storage and space that is cramped or shabby or uninspiring and badly lit. Take heart – there is always something you can do to improve both appearance and efficiency.

INSTANT REFRESHERS

/ / / On the simplest level a fresh coat of paint will work wonders. If ugly pipes and shabby storage are the problems, you could paint the whole lot in either a dark color, including the floor, or in a spanking white. This way, you will effectively hide all the shabbiness and at the same time provide a good background for food, cooking utensils, plants and accessories in bright, primary colors.

/ / / Dull-looking cabinets can be painted in high gloss or enamel, or even stencilled. Take off all old handles or knobs and replace with plain brass or a bright color like red or green.

/ / / If cabinet doors seem beyond redemption, you could leave them off altogether and have an open-shelved look, or replace them with louvered fronts or glass doors. You could hang easily

washable cotton or vinyl curtains in front, or blinds, which look neater.

/ / / You can retile the backsplash between cabinets and counter tops with plain white tiles (which are the least expensive) with colored grouting, or with a checkerboard of one other color and white. Or find a mixture of old tiles – even lovely old broken ones – to form a kind of patchwork or mosaic. If you cannot afford any sort of tile, or would rather spend the money on something else, you can cover the area with a self-adhesive plastic. Given a couple of coats of polyurethane sealer it becomes almost as hard as tiles. Do the same for a tired looking counter. If there are existing tiles which are worn or a disagreeable color, paint over them or pep them up by coloring the grouting in between with one of the new preparations on the market.

/ / / Alternatively, paper the walls with a wipe-able or washable vinyl paper, or a vinyl-coated paper, or an ordinary paper with an added couple of coats of polyurethane. The polyurethane varnish, available in gloss, matte or silk, might yellow the paper slightly so check first on an odd scrap.

/ / / Sometimes kitchen cabinets are in good condition but the counter tops are the worse for wear. Fix up the counters only. Add new laminated plastic tops or cover the old ones with butcher block, which is expensive but looks handsome for years if given regular coats of oil and is not exposed to too much water or heat. Or, if you are handy, use lengths of beech or other hardwood, butted together and edged with rounded beading. Give the surface at least three coats of yacht varnish rubbed down lightly with steel wool between coats.

/ / / Perk up the window. Paint the surround in a contrast color to the walls; add café curtains or a bright window shade; stretch glass or wood shelves across to display storage jars or nice pieces of glass or china, or a mixture, interspersed with herbs and plants in pots. Alternatively, stretch a wooden pole or an extension rod across the top and hang plants from it.

/ / / Old appliances like refrigerators, stoves, dishwashers and so on that have become scratched and battered can be resprayed white or a color with cans of car paint. If you use strips of masking tape, you can easily create stripes and diagonals and generally have fun. If the appliances are old anyway you might as well liven them up.

/ / / If the floor is awful but you can't afford to do much to it, paint it. Use gloss paint covered with a couple of coats of polyurethane. This works successfully with wood, old linoleum, vinyl and composition tiles. A little more money to spend? Then lay plywood in sheets or tiles and varnish it to look like cork.

/ / / Where deep shelving is out of the question go for shallow storage, one cup deep; even in a long, thin, galley kitchen it's possible to fit in a narrow shelf like this all along one wall. Take advange of the outer end-walls of cabinets to add more narrow shelves for spices or hooks for other utensils and implements. Attach similar shelves to the insides of cabinet doors.

/ / / Have extra workspace just where you want it with a butcher's block on wheels, preferably a double-decker providing extra storage on the lower deck. Some are equipped with hooks around the sides for even more storage.

/ / / If you can fix up an extra surface between cabinets, or across a corner, use this either for food preparation or as a desk. Make practical, rather than decorative use of the window, especially if there is no particular view outside, by putting shelves across. White or glass shelves will reflect a lot of light.

Strong colors in the kitchen but two very different effects. Red is a good choice: it is warm and welcoming and stimulates the appetite. An awkwardly shaped room (left) makes the most of a curving wall with bright red, built-in cabinets sobered by smart charcoal gray tiles. Warm natural wood and a profusion of carefully arranged dishes, cooking equipment and storage containers makes this a most welcoming kitchen. The hideaway kitchen (above) has a modern feel despite its collection of old containers. This strictly red, white and yellow scheme not only remains crisp and fresh, it also disappears behind folding doors when not in use.

Genuine country materials and textures will give you a fine country-style kitchen atmosphere. Here a traditional herringbone tiled floor has been combined with a sturdy wood top and brick peninsula and the obligatory scrubbed pine kitchen table for an authentic feel. The chain-hung pole and butcher's hooks have provided storage that also visually divides the room.

/ / / Are you desperate for extra storage and workspace? Then look up -- literally. There's a lot of space going unused up there. If the ceiling is a reasonable height, you can hang up a rack with hooks for storing pots and pans out of the way; they will free space below, yet equipment will be accessible. You can add high shelves above cabinets or extend storage units right up to the ceiling.

/ / / But storage isn't restricted to cabinets. Lots of open shelving looks businesslike and couldn't be more fashionable. Or you can attach poles and butcher's hooks at a convenient height above the work surface. Lightweight metal grids attached flat to the wall make good use of blank space that perhaps won't take shelves.

CABINETS ON A BUDGET

If a fully outfitted, streamlined kitchen made up of cabinets is what you have set your heart on, it's possible to achieve this on slim budget. If you are prepared to scour junk shops and secondhand shops and garage sales, you can probably find some decent cabinets that you can strip and stain or paint and equip with new handles. Watch for clearance sales of kitchen cabinets in big department stores, cabinet dealers, and home improvement centers; they often sell off their display kitchens at a big discount, usually when space must be made for a new line. If you ask, they will usually tell you what time of year this happens.

Unfinished wood cabinets that you can stain or paint yourself are good value. Office furniture stores sometimes provide cabinets that with a little ingenuity can easily be utilized in kitchens. Gym lockers, too, can be useful in kitchens as elsewhere in the house and can be painted or sprayed in cheerful colors to add to or create a special effect – perhaps an array of lockers each painted in a different primary color.

Maybe you've taken on a decently outfitted kitchen whose cabinets are in good shape, apart from worn and battered doors and drawer fronts. If that's all that's wrong, consider refacing them with new doors and drawer fronts. There are several

Kitchen storage need not be dull or expensive. These simple units (above) with their fine solid wood top, have been given a new identity by giving the cabinet fronts a dragged effect paint finish. And by creatively using large open baskets in existing niches (above right) an attractive, Mediterranean kitchen has resulted.

firms which specialize in refacing, which gives a kitchen a whole new look at a fraction of the price of completely new cabinets. You can even find firms who sell panels that can be fitted over your present doors – an easy, inexpensive way to effect a major change. Storage accessories for cabinet interiors, such as shelf units which fit inside doors or revolving racks for odd-shaped corner cabinets, can help double usable space.

If you decide that you want to start afresh with proper new cabinets, you should know that they are made up of three elements: the basic frame and shelves; the drawers and door fronts; and the work surface, which runs along the top of the base cabinets. Because price, quality, and features can vary a great deal, it's worth shopping around to get what you want. With less expensive units there's less choice in terms of widths of doors, but you can leave gaps between cabinets and span the space with countertop to give breakfast bar/tray space or room for washing machine, compact tumble dryer, wine rack or trash bin. Again, this might be a way to add your *own* touch, to give your kitchen a really individual look.

Ready-made cabinets come in a huge choice of finishes, colors, measurements and prices. Corner cabinets with a single door and either fixed or revolving shelves can be mounted across a corner which would ordinarily be simply dead space with the result that every spare bit of kitchen area is productively used.

Base units generally stand 36 inches from the floor, including the thickness of the counter, and widths match the overhead cabinets, though the depth is generally twice as much. You can buy them with drawers, doors, or both, with different depths for different drawers. Again, there are many refinements to choose from, like glide-out chopping boards, vegetable storage, wine racks, tray and cutlery racks, mixer stands, pot and saucepan lid racks, sliding trays for linen and cutlery racks, mixer stands, pot and saucepan lid racks, sliding trays for linen and so on. These sorts of sophisticated extras cost money but you can control your capital expenditure by buying standard but empty cabinets and filling them gradually as you can afford it, with 'space organizers' chosen to suit your particular needs from other kitchen storage specialists.

Food storage cabinets should be specially made to accommodate cans and jars and dry goods like breakfast cereals. Often they have doors that are particularly heavily hinged, with narrow shelving designed to hold a row of cans along the length of the doors for maximum storage capacity. They can usually be bought in overhead, base, or full-length models. Utility or broom closets are generally 12 to 24 inches deep, 7 feet tall and from 15 to 30 inches wide. They consist of one tall space with an upper shelf for storing cleaning supplies. Similar cabinets can be bought as housing units for particular built-in models of wall ovens and for refrigerators. Generally speaking, with the more reasonably priced brands of cabinetry, you will find there is less flexibility in terms of ranges of sizes and configurations.

GOOD ALTERNATIVES

You don't have to have cabinets. You can go for a high-tech kitchen with completely open storage if you use industrial shelving and wire grids available from hospital and catering supply stores. Or you can have a perfectly efficient and comfortable kitchen without cabinets or shelving, using any pieces of freestanding furniture you have, as long as you arrange them into a good work sequence with areas for food preparation, cooking, serving and washing dishes and somewhere for storage. There are lovely kitchens made from old cabinets, sideboards, even old armoires and even simpler kitchens that work beautifully and are little more than a tiled work surface and open pine shelving. They can look a lot more interesting and colorful than the expensive but ordinary-looking standard cabinets that you see everywhere.

White grid design with a natural wood trim (below) is smart but still has a homey feel. Wooden stools, the use of primary colors for accessories and provisions help create a friendly family kitchen.

White with wood trim again (right), but this time touches of black have added drama and sophistication. Black and white scheme has drawers have been cleverly balanced by careful accessorizing.

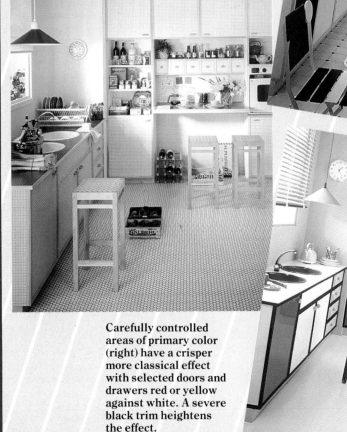

Carefully controlled areas of primary color (right) have a crisper more classical effect with selected doors and drawers red or yellow against white. A severe black trim heightens the effect.

One kitchen can look so many different ways depending on choice of trim and accessories. Here red and white looks fresh, smart and inviting, with a touch of buttercup yellow for added interest.

Strong colors need to be handled with restraint if they are to have most impact. Note how a simple red trim strengthens a speckled finish and is given just the right amount of emphasis by a couple of areas of pure color: red plain window shade, double sink and canisters.

A good variety of built-in storage makes the most of available space and remains flexible. Here, a good run of cabinets above and below is augmented by large and small drawers for all those kitchen odds and ends.

Kitchen floors need to be hardwearing, easy to clean and practical. This smart red and white grid design is printed on sturdy vinyl sheet flooring for easily mopped good looks. Ceramic tiles are an even hardier alternative, but aren't quite as warm and comfortable underfoot.

Good lighting over the sink helps make cleaning up less tedious and tiring.

In this kitchen a simple window shade over the window makes the most of natural light with a long flexed lamp directly overhead for after-dark illumination.

A smart, red mesh cart is not only useful for busy shopping trips, but also handy for moving heavy items around the kitchen. This one looks good enough to be stored on display.

A long legged chair or high stool converts a counter surface into a handy breakfast bar.

A large kitchen can sometimes be as difficult to plan successfully as a smaller one when cabinets are fitted naturally around the available wall areas, leaving a vast expanse of floor in the center. The best and most attractive solution is either a freestanding island unit, as shown here, or a peninsula adjoining a run of cabinets to create an 'E' shape. In this kitchen, where cooking is obviously treated as a serious business, a clean, white-tiled island unit provides plenty of storage and a variety of cooktop facilities. Built-in oven, refrigerator and pantry are streamlined into cabinets on the surrounding walls with more drawers and cabinets for storage and an illuminated preparation area. The white scheme is pristine and businesslike: cool white ceramic tiles on the floor and countertops, lots of white paint. Opaque glass windows let in plenty of natural light and eliminate the need for blinds or curtains.

WHAT ABOUT EQUIPMENT

It is rare to be able to buy all the big appliances one would like – refrigerator, freezer, range, dishwasher, washing machine, dryer, garbage disposer and so on – all at once, although if you want them, you should plan for them. Whether you are doing a kitchen from scratch or updating an old one, you must decide on your most pressing needs and leave space for the rest. Cooking and cleaning up are clearly priorities, so you'll need a stove and a sink before a washing machine.

Or instead of leaving empty spaces, go for stop-gaps with good reconditioned, secondhand or discontinued models that can be bought for a fraction of the cost of brand new ones. You have to be prepared for eventual breakdowns, but they'll tide you over for a while.

If you are thinking of expanding the household in any way, it is a good idea and more economical to choose larger rather than smaller appliances with an eye to the future.

If you are planning a major renovation in, say, six months or a year, you can improvise without large equipment in the meantime. An electric fry pan and crockpot can, together with perhaps a toaster oven and a sandwich maker, provide snacks, meals and a balanced diet until you can manage a new or reconditioned range. A microwave oven will enable you to prepare quick meals after an evening's decorating and work on the house; so will a pressure cooker. Any gadgets will be welcome in a newly outfitted kitchen when the work is done.

RANGES

If you are buying new, you can buy cooking equipment to suit practically every shape and size of kitchen, from separate cooktops and ovens to commercial freestanding ranges or even drop-in models that can be slipped into your cabinetry. Ceramic cooktops give the semblance of an almost unbroken work surface, and so do the new magnetic induction units (one version of which consists of individual decorative tiles), which do not heat up like burners because they use magnetic induction to cook by. Both cooktops are smooth in appearance and easy to clean, but ceramic cooktops can be dangerous if there are children in the household because it's difficult to tell if the burners are hot.

Some imported cooktops combine both gas and electric burners; others have interchangeable parts like a broiler, griddle and rotisserie. Some have built-in deep fryers, and there are stoves with both a conventional and a convection or a microwave oven. Other refinements are self-cleaning ovens; automatic ignition gas ranges without pilot lights; ovens with automatic timers, automatic meat thermometers for perfect roasts, commodious drawer space underneath for plate warming and for storing pots, pans and oven dishes; and tops with built-in

grills and their own cooking surface venting systems to carry away cooking odors.

Most freestanding ranges are about 24 inches deep and extend slightly beyond the average cabinet. Standard widths are 21 to 40 inches. Imported models will vary not only because European kitchens lack the space of American kitchens but also are designed in metric measurements. Whether you're considering imported or domestic equipment (the latter, of course, more readily available and less expensive but not always as flexible), usually you can choose between a single or double oven. Although most American models have the broiler at the bottom of the oven, bi-level models feature a small eye-level oven and broiler above the

burners. You will discover when you begin to comparison shop that freestanding ranges are a lot less expensive than separate cooktop and ovens, and they can be moved (or changed) later. You might also want to consider a drop-in range, which fits into the cabinetry.

Built-in ovens may be designed to go under the countertop, either beneath the cooktop or separated from it, or they may fit into cabinets at waist level so that they are more accessible. When you select a model, the literature should tell you the size of opening and the amount of ventilation you will need.

Compact imported cooktops are only 21 by 17 inches; domestic brands range from 30 to 42 inches wide. If you have space, always go for a larger model. Or, install two or three small cooktops in different parts of the kitchen. You can also install a combination of gas and electric burners.

Among the newer options are combination appliances that incorporate two or more conventional appliances into one, such as a cooktop, oven and dishwasher. These are most useful in small kitchens, where space is at a premium.

A microwave oven can be a blessing for working people with families to cook for, especially if used in conjunction with a freezer, There are now special browning versions of microwave ovens to ensure that the food doesn't come out looking pale, and the introduction of turntables means that you get even cooking. Microwave ovens are much smaller than

When space is short, furniture has to be flexible. This ingenious kitchen/dining table glides easily into the tiny galley kitchen for breakfasts and informal meals, and back into the dining area for more formal diners and parties. The overall scheme is kept simple: plain white with smoky brown ceramic tiles.

standard ovens, though built-in models often are the same width as conventional ovens. They are also available in space-saving models that can be mounted under the overhead cabinets.

REFRIGERATORS AND FREEZERS

These should depend on the size or potential size of your family and also on your lifestyle. A total of 12 cubic feet of refrigeration and freezer space is usually considered adequate for a couple. Add another cubic foot per person. If you can only shop once a week or so, you will need much more freezer space than if you could shop every day. If you cannot afford the space or money for a separate freezer – and most people in cities simply have not got the room – you should look at refrigerators with maximum freezer space and capacious food storage compartments. Bear in mind that a freezer doesn't necessarily have to fit into the kitchen: garage, cellar or service porch might be a better site. It's not unheard of to have a chest freezer in a little-used guest room. If you're hard up, you can't afford to be conventional, and the investment in a freezer will be repaid time and time again with savings on food.

Many refrigerator/freezer models have sealed meat and vegetable drawers with adjustable temperature and humidity controls to keep food fresher

longer. Frost-free models, which mean you never have to defrost, are as useful as self-cleaning ovens but use more energy. Additional luxuries now include ice water and crushed ice or ordinary ice dispensers, and even automatic ice-cream makers. Good refrigeration is an investment – it can save you time and money.

DISHWASHERS

On a budget? Yes, why not? Many people loathe doing dishes, begrudge the time spent on it and think a machine does a better job anyway. They would reckon it was money well spent. Efficient models will clean everything beautifully from fine glass to saucepans; they have settings that range from gentle to superscrub.

If you are a small family, choose a model with the sort of controls that allow you a rinse-and-hold cycle; this rinses dishes quickly, then allows them to stand until there's a full load to put through. Look for the kinds that have soft food disposal units to prevent blocked drains and which allow you to program the machine to start work after you have eaten. It's sometimes possible to save money by running your dishwasher (and/or your washing machine, for that matter) at off-peak hours for cheap electricity; enquire at your utility company for details.

A fold-down table and chairs quickly convert a corner of this warm, honey-toned kitchen into a smart breakfast area, yet leave the main area free for cooking.

The natural warmth of the wood trim on these otherwise plain, creamy beige units has been emphasized by a warm cork effect floor in easy-to-clean vinyl and a Liberty print shade at the window. The whole effect is freshened with built-in white appliances and a collection of bright china. A large window provides plenty of sill space for plants, flowers and favorite items which help screen a less than interesting view. Recessed downlights in the ceiling are the ideal back-up lighting system.

If you do not have space for a built-in model beside or under the sink, there are portables available on wheels. These can be rolled to the table for loading then rolled back to the sink to be connected to the taps and drains by hoses. Some have butcher block tops so that they can double as extra work tops and are convertible so that they can be built in later if you move. Most models are 24 inches wide to fit in with average countertop measurements.

SINKS AND GARBAGE DISPOSERS

Given the space – and the money – it is useful to have at least two sinks: one for soaking dishes, one for preparing vegetables and, ideally, a separate waste or garbage disposal unit. If you do have a garbage disposal, make absolutely sure you are hooked up to the sort of drainage system that will not be fouled up by liquid refuse in bulk. In some areas with septic systems, garbage disposers are illegal.

Have as much draining space as you can afford – a double drainer if possible. Some sinks are available with extra wood cutting board surfaces to fit across the top when necessary to provide extra work space; others have small spray attachments for easier cleaning. If you are very short of space look for corner sinks. Self-rimming sinks are better value

than drop-in sinks set into the countertop, as you don't then have the extra cost of the counter material.

The most popular choice for taps is a single swing spout with either one or two handles in stainless steel. The most popular sinks are made of porcelain-covered cast iron or of stainless steel. Sinks are also available made of vitreous enamel and molded plastic, and of Corian, a new marblelike plastic that is almost indestructible and that can be molded into a neat, all-in-one counter and sink. Corian sinks are not for kitchens where money is tight.

HOODS

Although some stoves have built-in self-venting outlets, there is an enormous market for hoods of every shape and description, with built-in fans for ventilation and to remove cooking smells. Most units need to be on an outside wall or ducted to vent outdoors but others are available which are ventless, recirculating the air through activated charcoal filters which should be changed regularly. All of them have incorporated light bulbs to give extra light over the cooktop. An extractor fan that can be fitted to a window is an economical alternative, but you should bear in mind that it tends to take heat from the kitchen on cold days.

The beauty of custom-made units is that they can be adapted to disguise features you'd rather not see. Here an awkwardly placed boiler has been neatly built into the cabinetry to create an interesting corner feature.

Coordinating the color accents was the final stage in planning this kitchen, where the blue and white fabric of the cafe curtain was carefully chosen to match the china pattern. Remnants of fabric have been used to make matching table linen.

The table is actually an inexpensive garden table covered with a long cloth and which can be folded away neatly when not in use. Wall cabinets to the ceiling make the most of available space.

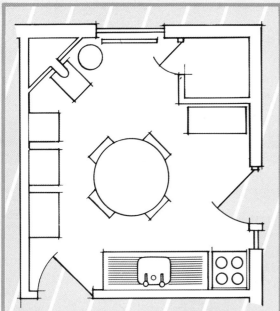

BEFORE: a walk-in pantry and prominent boiler made the room an awkward, difficult-to-plan shape. Appliances were slotted where they could be fitted in between cabinets; the sink and range were a good walk away from the main work area and had only a dull view of a blank wall beside a badly opening door to the rest of the house.

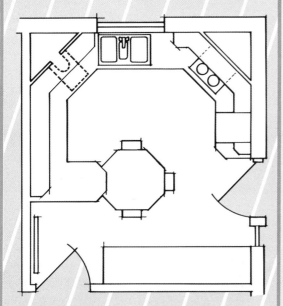

AFTER: the new kitchen plan has the walk-in pantry removed to make an easier, more regular shape to work with and the sink moved to a more sensible – and interesting – position under the window with a view of the garden. Appliances are now placed far more logically and the ugly boiler hidden inside a specially designed corner unit. An L-shaped peninsula defines the kitchen work area and provides extra storage on both sides; now that the kitchen door has been rehung, these cabinets are perfect for storing all household linen as they have been positioned to be easily accessible to the rest of the house.

A t first sight this family kitchen seemed too awkward to imbue with the sleek efficiency and photogenic charm of the pictures in the brochures. The room itself was a good size but irregular, mostly thanks to a large walk-in pantry in one corner and, a more recent thoughtless addition by previous owners, an unattractive boiler which stuck out awkwardly into the room. A random arrangement of cabinets provided pitifully small additional storage facilities and the sink was positioned unusually with its back to the window and facing a blank wall.

It was a room which obviously needed a complete rethinking, if it was to work efficiently as kitchen and family breakfast room; the owner had a clear idea in his head of how he wanted it to be and the facilities it should offer, but was doubtful if it would ever work in a room such as this. However, many drawn-up plans and calculations later, the dream seemed a possibility at last.

Obviously the pantry had to go, making the room a more regular rectangular shape and also providing badly needed extra floor space. In addition a radiator under the window was removed, thus allowing a continuous run of cabinets that could be built around that awkward boiler. An L-shaped peninsula was intended to provide not only interest and extra storage, but also a natural place to put the table for informal family meals, while base and wall cabinets running right around the room would supply more storage and counter space than was hoped possible.

Perfectly satisfied with the revised layout of his new kitchen, the owner found himself in a dilemma over the cabinets: should he go for a traditional country kitchen atmosphere or something a little sleeker and more sophisticated now that the children were growing up? He decided to opt for the best of both worlds and chose pure white for everything – cabinets, tiles, sink, appliances, even flooring; that way he could dress it up whichever way the fancy took him. These pictures show how stunning a simple touch of pink can be – it could quite easily be changed to red, yellow, blue, green or even black with very little effort. A few traditional touches and the warmth of wood create a farmhouse atmosphere (see previous page). Bearing cost in mind, it makes sense to choose a style you can live with.

Plain neutral cabinets provide the perfect background for bright accessories, which can be changed relatively easily.

A peninsula is useful for breaking up large areas and providing extra storage. Here roomy cabinets are handy for storage.

It is always those small final details which bring out the best in a kitchen and it is worth taking the time and trouble to choose them carefully. Here white sink and appliances are fitted into the scheme perfectly, while a white floor is more practical than it seems when it is easy-to-wipe, hard-wearing vinyl. Look for clever, space-saving ideas in your cabinets too, such as these handy deep drawers and the wine rack which fills an awkward gap. A window shade (below) provides a useful (and easily replaced) splash of pure color).

A ventilation unit is not only essential over the cooktop to remove fumes and steam; many are fitted with a useful light.

Appliances are fitted to a logical sequence: refrigerator under the preparation area left; sink and dishwasher; cooktop and oven.

Open shelving interspersed among the wall cabinets adds interest and variety and the chance to display favorite items.

A plain white table echoes the curve of the kitchen cabinets and offers flexible seating arrangements for informal meals.

White ceramic tiles make an easy-to-clean backsplash, an affordable luxury when you consider that the area to cover is small.

BATHROOMS

Like the kitchen, the bathroom needs a lot of thought. Whatever the size of the space and your budget, whether you have in mind a practical, hygienic washing place or something far more luxurious, you will still need: bath and/or shower; basin or sink; toilet; well-lit mirror; at least one chair or stool; towel rails – heated if possible; hooks on the back of the door for clothes; adequate storage space for cosmetics, shaving gear, medicines, soap and toiletries, comfortable, practical flooring and a generous backsplash area.

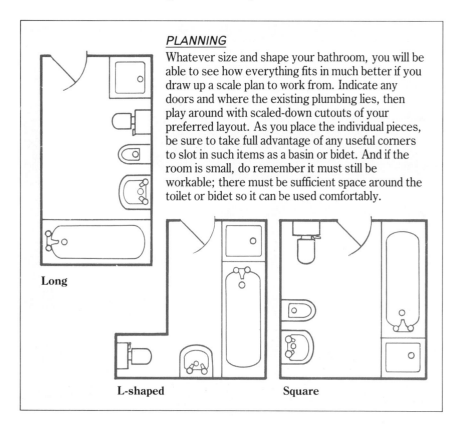

PLANNING

Whatever size and shape your bathroom, you will be able to see how everything fits in much better if you draw up a scale plan to work from. Indicate any doors and where the existing plumbing lies, then play around with scaled-down cutouts of your preferred layout. As you place the individual pieces, be sure to take full advantage of any useful corners to slot in such items as a basin or bidet. And if the room is small, do remember it must still be workable; there must be sufficient space around the toilet or bidet so it can be used comfortably.

Long

L-shaped

Square

If more than one person needs to use the bathroom at the same time, a double basin is a real boon. This one fits neatly into a double vanity unit with mirrored wall above to combine washing and grooming facilities with plenty of cabinet area, in the minimum space.

PLACING EQUIPMENT

If you are starting a bathroom from the beginning or doing a conversion, consider whether more than one person is ever going to be using the room at the same time. Clearly it is quite impractical – and expensive – to have more than one of most items, but there is no reason why you shouldn't have a double basin and vanity unit if you can fit them in. They do ease the pressure at rush hours. In a large area, washbasins or sinks look better and are more practical if they can be set into a cabinet with storage underneath.

If the room is really spacious, a freestanding bath in the middle of the floor or on a platform looks good. There is no reason why a bath should be huddled up in the corner, except for the convenience of the plumber.

Mirrors need to be large, well-lit and as free as possible from fogging. This should not be too difficult if the bathroom is well heated and ventilated, but there are various mirrored cabinets available and also mirrors with built-in lights or bulbs all around like theatrical mirrors, which warm the glass and so eliminate condensation. If you prefer to use an old mirror, have swing arm lights at the side, or attach strips of theatrical bulbs at the top or sides. Make sure that they are operated by a pull cord or that you have a bathroom circuit breaker. Safety regulations about electricity in bathrooms must be observed. If you are buying a bathtub, first do as much research as possible unless you are trying to get a secondhand one, which is certainly the cheapest thing to do. Buying new gives you a vast range of shapes to choose from – oval, octagonal, curved, old-fashioned with claw feet. Steam baths, whirlpool massage baths, hot tubs, Jacuzzis, and bathtubs big enough for two are too expensive for slim budgets unless you can buy them secondhand.

Clever lighting and mirrors are your allies when trying to work a little bathroom magic. What is really a small room (center) appears very large with the profussion of plants and freestanding tub reflected in textured mirrors on every bit of wall space. This sink area (left) becomes larger than life with a large mirror surrounded by strip lights.

When you find a design
you like, why not let it
spread itself a little. The
plain deep blue and white
bathroom below was
given a touch of
excitement with a fun
shower curtain which
worked well when
expanded beyond the bath
to become a wall border.

Blue again (bottom), but
this time a rich
Wedgewood blue and
white room with built-in
cabinets. These not only
look sleek and smart;
they also hide all the
plumbing as well as
providing a useful area
for much needed storage
space.

By creating a 'dead' space in this bathroom, not only have the pipes and plumbing been effectively hidden from sight, but a useful shelf area has also resulted. This provides a useful place for both open storage of practical items, such as soap and toothbrushes, and display of the little 'treasures' that give the room life.

Basically, the more conventional baths are 5 feet long by 2 feet 6 inches wide, but you can buy many shapes, including lengths from 4 feet 11 inches to 5 feet 11 inches to 6 feet. If space is very tight, you can find corner baths, or soaking rather than lying tubs, which measure about 4 feet 7 inches by 2 feet 4 inches or 4 feet square. It's important to know all these measurements because every inch might count. But whatever the size and color of the bath you choose, try to get one with handles at the side. It's safe and helpful for children and elderly people as well as a great blessing for those who are pregnant, have back trouble or feel frail and unsteady after or during an illness. The cheapest and most common material for baths is acrylic, which can be moulded easily to incorporate seats, soap dishes, bath rests and so on. Water stays hotter in acrylic than metal baths, but acrylic scratches easily. If this happens, get the surface really dry, then rub the scratch down with metal polish and rinse off thoroughly. Acrylic also burns easily and can be damaged by nail polish, varnish remover, some dry cleaning fluids and cigarettes. See that acrylic baths are installed according to the manufacturer's instructions or they may not remain rigid.

Cast iron with a porcelain enamel finish is the classic but most expensive material for baths and still holds its own because it is fairly stain-free. Fiberglass baths are made of layers of Fiberglass bonded together with polyester resin. They are much stronger and more rigid than the acrylic variety and come in a wide range of colors, including metallic and pearlized finishes.

If you have an energy-saving shower head installed, showers are water- and energy-saving because they take less water than is needed for a bath. They are also quick and invigorating. If you connect them to an instantaneous water heater that heats only the water actually used, they are even more economical. They also take up comparatively little room – one square yard of floor space, and so can be installed in all sorts of odd corners, provided there is a water supply and drainage nearby.

If you have a shower built in you will need a mixer valve and shower head and a ceramic, steel or acrylic shower tray. Install them in a corner or recess, cover the walls with tiles and install a glass door or screen or shower curtain according to your pocket. It is easy to put in a shower above a bathtub, again screening it off with a glass panel or shower curtains. You can often get much prettier effects by using ordinary cotton fabric or terrycloth with a separate clear plastic curtain behind – pretty enough to be admired, practical enough to get wet.

Basins or sinks can be freestanding, wall hung, partially supported by front legs or sunk in a vanity unit. They are available in the same finishes as tubs and in all sorts of shapes and sizes according to taste, size and pocket. Taps or faucets and other hardware should be chosen at the same time as you choose your bathtubs and basins; they can be as expensive as the basin itself. Again there is a huge choice from stainless steel through brightly colored plastic to the more luxurious and more costly brass and porcelain.

Two fantasy bathrooms show just how stunning the room can be if you let your imagination run free. Far left an arched niche makes the perfect setting for a font style basin with a big brass tap like a drinking fountain. A weathered effect mosaic of tiles on the floor only reinforces the image and with mirror, towel rails and shelves for soaps and toiletries, the grotto is completely self-contained. The bigger bathroom (left) also aims to focus attention on an unusual basin, this time an elegant freestanding model, in a modern tubular design complete with integral mirror, towel rail, soap dish and toothbrush holder. A wooden slatted blind and giant palm create a good backdrop framed by a bold border of tiles. Black bath and towel stand balance the effect dramatically.

Toilets are generally wall-hung or the pedestal variety and come as low as 9 inches from the floor or considerably higher and in a variety of widths. You can buy seats in colors to match the toilet itself or get beautifully made wooden ones, sometimes with cane tops, which have become very popular again.

Tiles come in an enormous number of designs and colors now, but the cheapest are the plain whites or creams. You can make them more interesting by using colored grouting or by making a border all around the tub and under the ceiling. Sometimes you can buy thin lengths of plain border tile or tiles specially made as borders. Or use halves of normal tiles. It would be very expensive to tile a bathroom completely; most are half-tiled but you can get away with less. Two rows of tiles above bath and basin are adequate. Decorate the rest of the room with a washable wallpaper; it's easier to change when you tire of it, and it looks less clinical. In a half-tiled room, you can add a wallpaper or vinyl border above the tiles. Cheaper still would be to paint the walls with a semigloss paint.

STORAGE

Well-thought-out storage in a bathroom will, or should, get rid of any unappealing clutter of tooth-brushes, paste, cleaners and soggy towels. Vanity units will cope with a greal deal, including bottles of shampoo, hot water bottles, toilet paper and tissues, while generous towel rack and cabinet space will take care of the rest. You can always curtain off a basin and hide a lot of stuff behind that. Try to fit in storage anywhere and everywhere you can, even if it is the narrowest of cabinets with shelves only one bottle deep. See any available space as a potential storage area.

COSMETIC IMPROVEMENTS

Not many people have the chance to plan a bathroom from the beginning or even have the possibility of changing things around. You are pretty well stuck with what is there and the only solution is to change the things that can be changed, including the atmosphere of the bathroom.

Good heating and lighting will work marvels. So will comfortable flooring. In what is generally a small area consider carpet – there are types made especially for bathrooms – sealed cork tiles or beautiful ceramic tiles. You won't need many tiles and you could find them at discount shops. Wallpaper pasted over walls and ceilings, put on bath panels and even on flush doors, edged and held in with narrow beading, works an immediate change for the better, especially if it is given a coating or two of clear lacquer or polyurethane. Papered bath panels can be safeguarded with transparent adhesive vinyl or you can use vinyl for the panels. Never underesti-mate the power of plain paint in white or a good strong color. Some of the best bathrooms are completely white: white walls, equipment, floor, painted cane chairs, white towels, shower curtains and shade. Colored taps and plants add just the right accent.

If you choose a dark warm color of paint it will certainly hide things like ugly plumbing and tangled pipes and provide a good background for prints, photographs and attractive odds and ends to be massed on the walls and shelves. You might do something daring and make a feature of the offending pipework by painting it a strong primary color against white or yellow walls.

Even if you cannot change the decoration in, say, a rented apartment, you can still make an enormous difference with plants, good towels and a rug or nylon carpet. A nasty looking basin can be disguised with a skirt of fabric to match a new shade. Ugly tiles can be painted over. If you can't afford beautifully colored towels, you can make plain white ones look more interesting by adding a border of a vivid contrasting color. This is a good way to restore the looks to a towel that is fine in the middle but frayed at the edges.

Storage can be a problem in small bathrooms; towels and dirty linen are bulky items and toiletries or medical items need to be readily available. Built-in shelves and cabinets will make the best use of any spare wall space or wasted corners and failing that, freestanding cabinets, shelves, baskets and even carts provide invaluable storage facilities where they can be fitted in. Clever built-in shelves (left top) have been cleverly incorporated in a cabinet designed to hide the pipework for an over-bath shower attachment, then painted to match the room. The tiny bathroom (left below) has a useful and decorative strip of brass pegs beneath a bathroom cabinet with both shelf and cabinet storage, to provide a convenient place to hang towels, clothes, etc. A floor-to-ceiling shelf unit (left) provides ample storage for towels, toiletries and dirty linen in a relatively small space and is cleverly concealed from view by smart striped window shades – cheaper and better space savers than hinged doors.

This bathroom is not exactly generous – it is just big enough for bath, basin and toilet. It has already been half tiled and has one small window. Yet how different it can look simply by treating it in different ways! Replacing the bathroom fixtures and wall tiles is often a hasty and expensive move even if you can afford it. It is always worth appraising what you have first and seeing if a little imagination and a few new accessories can effect a convincing transformation.

Here new taps and towels, a little paint or woodstain and a change of flooring convert this plain white bathroom to Edwardian dignity, a comfortable conservatory or stark modernity with the minimum of expense. Note, too, those little final touches such as pictures and plants, which make all the difference.

Mahogany wood stain, a few lengths of beading and a brass handle transform this vanity unit and bath panel to Edwardian splendor when teamed with a rich burgundy carpet and magnificent brass taps and shower attachment. Floor-length curtains are brown terrycloth hung on a mahogany-stained pole. Accessories such as mirrors, toilet seat, toothbrush holder and towel rail are also mahogany.

Fresh, clean and bright, this scheme has been stripped back to basics using plain white as a major scheme and simply adding touches of brilliant yellow and a splash of blue for warmth and interest. This kind of project should only be attempted if fixtures and tiles are in excellent condition: nothing can be disguised. Against the plain white background a little color is most effective.

White painted trellis from garden centres costs very little and hides a multitude of sins from uneven walls to cracked tiles you can't afford to replace. Here it as been hung with trailing plants to create a pleasant conservatory atmosphere.

Basin and bath have been inexpensively boxed in and painted – useful for stencilling and tiling too, or staining for a natural wood effect (see Edwardian style bathroom, left).

The floor area in most bathrooms is usually so minimal you can afford to splurge on something expensive such as good-looking carpet, or as here, stylish ceramic tiles available in a wide range of styles and colors and special non-slip finishes.

A simple white fabric shade is sufficient to screen the window here with lots of leafy plants to provide extra cover. Replacing the glass with frosted or opaque glass or even a mirror would be equally effective.

If you have the space, some form of seating is an invaluable asset in the bathroom for painting toenails or putting on socks. Here a wicker chair fits the conservatory theme. In the Edwardian bathroom (left) it has been painted white.

Those keen on complete color coordination will find plenty of scope in the bathroom. Here soaps, towels, bathrobe and even slippers have all been carefully chosen to suit the scheme.

You only have to look at an exposed rock face, worn down, pitted and eaten away, to realize the effect extremes of weather can have on the bricks and mortar and wood of your home. Regular maintenance of the exterior can seem like an expensive and awkward chore and it is tempting to put it off until the next year or until it shows more signs of wear – false economy when you consider the cost of repairing a building that has been allowed to decay or reach the point of dereliction. Roof, walls, gutters and woodwork must be protected from the ravages of sun, wind, wet and freezing conditions before they make inroads into the actual fabric and incur expensive repair and replacement bills, preferably at the end of the warmest summer months when everything has dried out, and in preparation for the winter. It will be time and money well spent, not only as an investment for your own comfort and security, but for a potentially good resale price too.

If you live in a condo or coop, the building should be regularly maintained as part of the maintenance fee. It is worth checking these details at the outset and establishing where responsibility lies for repair of roofs, foundations, masonry, woodwork and so on, and to make sure such arrangements are adhered to. In a single-family home, total responsibility falls fairly and squarely on your own shoulders and it is up to you to keep a weather eye open for likely points of decay. If you are thinking of doing the work yourself, it is important to keep safety in mind: working 20 feet or more up is dangerous, and if you must use a ladder, make sure you have someone available to hold it for you and buy one of those clip-on ladder trays to hold paint cans or roller tray, brushes, etc. Far better and safer is to buy or rent a proper scaffolding system, which is light, easy to erect and allows you complete, easy freedom of movement across the width of the building.

Gutters and woodwork are the items which need the most regular, at least annual, maintenance. A blocked or leaking gutter leads to damp walls and a multitude of other, expensive problems, so make sure they are free of any debris by cleaning thoroughly once or twice a year, definitely in the autumn when they tend to fill with leaves and feathers. Cracks and broken brackets can usually be repaired by painting with a sealant or replacing sections of guttering fairly cheaply. Wood siding and woodwork on windowsills and doors soon shows the effects of weathering, especially when south-facing, where strong sunlight will crack and blister paint or varnish. Before winter every year, sand to remove any loose paint or splinters and repaint, making sure the wood is perfectly dry: sealed-in moisture will only rot the wood.

Walls and brickwork should be able to withstand the effects of weathering for several years unless they are in an exposed coastal location. Look out for crumbly or missing pointing between the bricks; if this has started to decay it will have to be redone which means laboriously scraping out the old mortar and repointing. Finishes such as pebble dash and

paints will help preserve the exterior longer if properly applied.

Never wait until your roof leaks to remind you it needs maintaining – replace lost tiles or shingles as soon as you spot them missing and check that chimney's are secure and well pointed. If the whole roof is in poor condition it is more sensible in the long run to have the whole area retiled than to attempt to patch it.

Keeping gardens, backyard, driveways and paths in good repair helps maintain the overall condition of your house too: not just psychologically but in a practical way too since rubbish, rubble and unruly foliage piled against the house will lead to damp, termites and erosion.

This house has been pitifully neglected. Roof tiles were loose and in a bad state of repair; window and door frames needed to be restored and repainted – if not totally replaced; the garden had become overgrown and unsightly. A new owner gave it the treatment the house so desperately needed, from replacing the roof to clearing the whole garden.

Safety and security in the home are sadly often undervalued or overlooked until disaster draws them to attention. It is sheer foolhardiness not to fit proper locks to doors both at the back and front of the house, and window locks on all the windows. Make sure these can be opened quickly and easily in an emergency, particularly if the windows are double glazed. Many new windows these days are fitted with automatic locks hidden in the frame which allows them to be fixed open at a crack for ventilation. Otherwise, window locks are relatively cheap and easy to fit.

It is a good idea to contact your local police station for advice about home security. Police will be glad to come to your home and give advice on the best locks and security devices for your particular circumstances. There is a wide range of burglar alarm systems on the market, from the simple alarm bell activated by a forced door or window, to a highly sophisticated computerized system that activates lights or buzzers by sensing the body heat of intruders; they are an effective deterrent but not cheap to buy and install. A good outdoor light front and rear will deter the casual break-in at night; the rest is common sense: don't leave windows open when you go out, keep tools and ladders locked away and take special precautions when you go away – cancelling papers, asking police and neighbors to keep an eye on the place and pick up mail. Special timers that turn on lights at irregular intervals are a good investment if you are often out in the evenings.

Safety inside the home is again a matter of common sense: no slippery rugs and mats; check stair carpets regularly for loose rails and tacks; have electrical appliances regularly serviced; never overload electrical outlets – install more if you need them; and keep a well-stocked medicine cabinet for emergencies. The kitchen and bathroom are prime accident areas; saucepan handles should be placed where they cannot get caught or pulled off and beware of steam – as lethal as any open flame. A fire blanket within reach of the stove with smother an accidental flare-up and if you have an extinguisher, make sure it is within reach and a decent size – those no bigger than an aerosol can are useless. Always wipe up and dry spills immediately.

Bathrooms should be made as non-slip as possible and if you can, outfit the bath with some kind of handle grips. Electrical outlets should be equipped with ground fault outlets and the light should be resistant to moisture.

To reduce risk of fire, check wiring regularly and never leave an open fire unattended without a fireplace screen.

Finally, whether you plan to have a family within the near future or you have visitors with small children, you might like to know you can get special guards for the top of your stove to prevent pots and pans from being pulled or knocked off. Also, you can have small folding gates installed at the top and bottom of staircases.

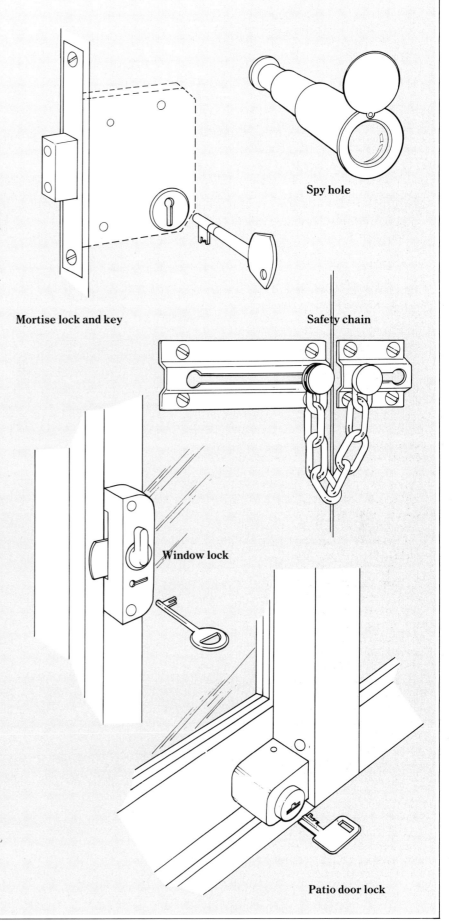

Spy hole

Mortise lock and key

Safety chain

Window lock

Patio door lock

ACCENT COLORS
Contrast colors used to spice up room schemes and to draw attention to chosen objects.

ACCENT LIGHTING
Decorative lighting which is used to draw attention to chosen objects, and to create moods and highlights.

ACOUSTIC TILES
Ceiling tiles which absorb sound. They are made from prefinished slotted insulation board or from styrofoam or Fiberglass.

AIRBRICK
A perforated brick set into a wall to allow ventilation.

ARCHITRAVE
A moulded or decorated band framing a panel or an opening such as a door.

AUSTRIAN BLIND
Ruched blind which is also known as a festoon blind, pull-curtain or balloon shade. It has rows of vertical shirring and can be raised and lowered by cords threaded through rings which are attached to the back of the shade at regular intervals. This type of shade can be made from scratch or from a kit.

BAFFLE
A narrow screen or partition placed so as to hinder or control the passage of light or sound.

BALANCE
Arrangement of objects around an imaginary central point to achieve a pleasing result. Balance can either be symmetrical (where objects on one side of the 'point' are mirrored by those on the other) or asymmetrical (in which case they are not).

BALLOON BLIND
A shade or blind with deep inverted pleats which create a billowing, balloon-like effect. Like an Austrian blind it is pulled up and down by cords threaded through rings attached to the back.

BANQUETTE
A long, upholstered seat, frequently built in along one side of a wall.

BATISTE
A fine fabric like cambric.

BEVEL
A process whereby surface edges are cut to slant e.g. on wood, glass or worktops.

BUCKRAM
A stiffened linen cloth. More often, Petersham is used.

BULLETIN BOARD
A board, often made from cork, on which papers or pictures can be attached.

BURLAP
A coarse sacking material (may be known as hessian).

BUTCHER'S BLOCK
A continuous run of thick wood or a wooden block with legs such as butchers use in their shops. Both are useful for chopping and preparing meat and vegetables.

CAFÉ CURTAIN
A short curtain hung from a rod halfway up a window as in French cafés. It is sometimes hung in a double tier.

CANE
Slender, flexible, woody stems, split into narrow strands and woven into chair backs and seats and also used to make blinds.

CASEMENT WINDOW
A window that opens on vertical hinges.

CERAMIC TILES
Fired clay tiles with a very hardwearing glaze. There is a large range of colors, patterns, textures and sizes.

CHAIR OR DADO RAIL
Wooden molding, lengths of which can be attached to the wall to stop chair backs from rubbing the decoration.

CHINTZ
A cotton fabric printed in several colors on a light or white background.

CHIPBOARD
Board with an inner core of compressed softwood chips and resin. More often particleboard.

CONSOLE TABLE
A small rectangular table, longer than it is wide, usually set against the wall.

CORIAN
A marble-like plastic substance used for sinks or worktops. It can be molded, is durable and almost completely stain-resistant.

CORNICE
A decorative horizontal band of plaster, metal or wood used to surmount a wall or to conceal curtain fixtures.

CORONA
A crown-shaped projection above a bed from which drapery is hung.

COSMETIC DECORATION
Purely decorative alteration as opposed to structural alteration. It is usually done solely to improve appearance.

COVING
A curved molding or join connecting the ceiling and wall.

DADO
The lower part of a wall separated by a rail known as the dado or chair rail.

DECK PAINT
A strong, dense paint used to paint boat decks. It is very tough and hardwearing. Also known as marine or yacht paint.

DHURRIE
An Indian cotton carpet. This type of carpet is also useful as wall hangings and throws on furniture.

DIMMER SWITCH
A knob (or reostat) or fingertip control panel used to control brightness of light.

DORMER WINDOW
A vertical window set into a sloping roof.

DOWNLIGHTS
Light fixtures that can be mounted or recessed into a ceiling. Their effect is to cast pools of light onto the wall, objects or seating below.

DRAGGING
A painting technique which gives a subtle effect to a large wall surface, cabinets or furniture. Paint is applied in a thin wash in vertical strokes with an almost dry brush in a contrasting or darker/lighter shade to the base coat.

ECLECTIC
To choose from various sources; not following any one system but selecting from and using the best components of several styles.

EPHEMERA
A collection of objects, not necessarily valuable, such as old posters and theater programs

ERGONOMICS
The study of work patterns and conditions, in order to achieve the maximum degree of efficiency.

ETAGÈRE
A set of open shelves supported by columns or corner posts.

FAUX BOIS
An artificial wood effect on a surface achieved by painting and graining.

FESTOON BLIND
Similar to an Austrian blind but rather more elaborate.

FRAMING PROJECTOR
A light fitting whose beam can be shaped accurately so that a given surface, such as a painting, table top or collection of items, can be lit exactly.

FRIEZE
A decorative horizontal band or border along a wall or dado.

GALLEY KITCHEN
Small and narrow, like the kitchen in a ship or boat.

GROUTING
Filling up or finishing joints between tiles with a thin mortar. The name of the powder or ready-mixed product.

HALF-TESTER
A small canopy or tester over a bed, covering only the pillow end.

HESSIAN
A coarsely woven cloth, also known as burlap.

HI-TECH
Contemporary style adapting industrial components for domestic use.

HOB
The stove top. The surface on which pans are heated. It is sometimes separate from the oven, and set into a worktop.

HOURGLASS CURTAINS
Curtains stretched between two rods (fixed at top and bottom of the window) and tied in the middle to show a triangle of window on either side.

ISLAND UNIT
In kitchen, a fixed, freestanding unit. It can have any combination of sink, stove and countertop, with storage underneath.

LACQUER
A durable varnish which is applied in layers and then polished to a mirror-like finish.

LOUVERS
A series of overlapping slats which filter or exclude light while allowing ventilation.

MAKING GOOD
To repair as new.

MARBLING
A painting technique which gives a veined, marble-like appearance to a surface.

MATCHSTICK BLIND
A blind made with fine sooden sticks which are stitched together.

MATTE FINISH
A completely flat finish, with no shine or luster.

MEXICAN TILES
Ceramic tiles whose colors and patterns are inspired by traditional Mexican designs.

MOIRÉ
The wavy design on silk, or other fabrics, which gives a watered appearance.

MONOCHROMATIC SCHEME
Design using one basic color as its theme, in a variety of shades and textures.

MURPHY BED
A bed that is let down from the wall against which it is concealed when not in use.

OTTOMAN
Technically, a long, low upholstered seat with no back; alternatively, a circular seat divided into four, with a central back. More commonly, a large upholstered footrest, often matching a chair.

PARQUET
A form of wooden flooring where the grain of one square runs at right angles to that in the adjacent square.

PARSON'S TABLE
A square or rectangular table with wide straight legs.

PEDESTAL TABLE
A table supported by a central, single post.

PEGBOARD
A board (usually Masonite) perforated with holes from which pegs can be attached. Can be mounted on a kitchen wall and used for hanging utensils.

PENDANT LIGHT
A light fitting suspended from the ceiling.

PENINSULAR UNIT
A unit that juts out into a room and can be approached from three sides.

PILLOW SHAMS
Covers for pillows to match the bed coverings, when pillows are propped on top of the bed. They often have a ruffle running along the whole outside edge.

PINHOLE LIGHTING
A spotlight fitting through which a narrow beam of light is projected, the beam spreading widely downward.

QUARRY TILES
Fired tiles made from unrefined clay, which provide very durable flooring.

RAG ROLLING
Decorative technique of creating patterns with a rag on a wet painted surface.

REVEAL (EMBRASURE)
The sides of a window between the frame and the outer surface of the wall.

RISE-AND-FALL FITTING
Used to adjust the height of a pendant light, especially when it is hung over a table.

ROMAN BLIND
A blind that draws up into neat horizontal folds by means of cords threaded through rings attached at regular intervals to the back of the fabric.

SASH CURTAINS
A piece of fabric or curtain panel with rod pockets at top and bottom. Ordinary brass or tension rods are then threaded through and mounted at both top and bottom of the window to stretch the curtain between them.

SCRAP-SCREEN
Popular in the Victorian era, this was made of hinged panels onto which scraps and cutouts were pasted then varnished over.

SKIRTING OR BASEBOARD
Traditional wooden band running along the base of a wall as a protection against kicking and scuffing.

STENCIL
A decorative design which is cut out of cardboard or acetate, then reproduced onto a surface below with paint using a stencil brush or spray gun.

STIPPLING
Speckled effect to wall painting, using a paint-soaked sponge.

SWAG AND TAIL
Elaborate valance-like treatment for curtains. The fabric is caught near each end so that the middle part, or swag, falls in a graceful curve and the ends hang in tails.

SWIRLING
Method of painting top coat allowing the undercoat to show through.

TESTER
A wood or fabric canopy covering the whole bed area.

TRACK LIGHTING
A length of track along which a number of light fittings are suspended and supplied by one electrical outlet.

UPLIGHTS
Accent lights which are placed on the floor. They can be concealed behind sofas and plants to give dramatic effects.

VALANCE
A decorative horizontal band of fabric usually attached to the top of the window frame or just above, to hide rods and provide added interest.

VENETIAN BLIND
A pull-up blind made from horizontal slats that can exclude light completely or filter it.

WALLWASHERS
Angled downlights or uplights that bathe the walls or walls and ceiling with light.

WINDOW SHADE
A fabric blind which is controlled by a string mechanism. May be used on storage instead of doors.

WORK TRIANGLE
An imaginary line linking the work areas around the sink, stove and refrigerator.

YACHT PAINT
A tough, hardwearing paint, also known as deck paint, used on boats or to paint wooden floors.

ACKNOWLEDGEMENTS / / / / / / / / / /

The author would like particularly to thank: the editors, Renny Harrop and
Elizabeth Longley, for all their input, help and patience; the designers,
Mary Evans and Judith Highton; and her long-suffering assistants,
Sarah Allen and Annabel Longworth.

The publishers would to thank:
Sarah Lifton, for her editorial assistance.

Bredero Homes Limited, for use of their Tweed Bungalow for original room
designs and photography as featured on pages, 46/7, 68/9, 82/3, 84/5,
92/3, 104/05 and 112/13.

Massey Construction Limited for work carried out on the Tweed Bungalow.

The publishers would like to thank the following for their co-operation in providing merchandise for special photography:

All Our Yesterdays, pine mirror 118/19; Amtico, vinyl flooring 68/9, 106, 108/09; And So to Bed…, bedstead & cushions 56/7; Armstrong, vinyl floor tiles 104/05; ASB Marketing, Bauhaus chairs 14/15, swivel chairs 76/7; Laura Ashley, fabric 106; Axminster Carpets, carpet (Brixham Turkey) 46/7; wicker hampers 14/15, accessories 36/7, table mats 39, tablecloth & napkins, rattan chairs & vases 64/5, ceramic plant pots 82/3, 92/3, 104/05, table mats, apron, oven mitts, cutlcry, glasses, storage jars 108/09; Carousel, blinds, 82/3, 92/3, 104/05, 112/13; Collins & Hayes, sofa 76/7; Covent Garden General Store, baskets 14/15, brassware & accessories 36/7, tea pots & china, plant baskets 64/5, suitcases 76/7, china duck 112/13; Crabtree & Evelyn, tioletries 112/13, 118/19; Crayonne, accessories 112/13, yellow accessories 118; Crown Paints, 14/15, 36/7, 46/7, 56/7, paint and floor cloth 64/5, 76/7, 82/3, 84/5, 92/3, 104/05, 112/13, 118/19; Elizabeth David, coffee maker 46, kitchen equipment & accessories 104/05, kitchen accessories 106, kitchen accessories, saucepans, cruets & condiments 108/09; Derwent Upholstery, dining table 14/15; Descamps, tablecloths 56/7, dressing gown & towels 76/7, 118/19; Designers Guild, wickerwork, cushions & ceramics 64/5, applique cushions 84/5; Dorma, bed linen 46, 56/7, 76/7, table napkins 85, bed linen 92/3; David Douglas Carpets, rag rug 56/7, Cream rug 84/5; Dulux, painted floors 36/7, 38, 39, stained floor 56/7, 64/5; paint 106, 108/09, mahogany stain 118; Philip Edwards, wallpaper 82/3, 84/5; Robin & Mary Ellis, dining table 82/3, small round table 84/5; Englishman's Castle, green felt 46/7, blinds, tablecloth & cushions 82/3, blinds, window seat, cushions & tablecloths 84/5, blind & shower curtain (fabric Boras Wafveri) 112/13; The Fire Place, fireplaces 14/15, 36/7, 38, 39; Freemans Focus catalogue, bed linen 38; Garfield Glass, mirrors 14/15, 36/7, 38; General Trading Company, umbrella stand 68/9, plants & baskets 82/3, small tables, planters, candlesticks 84/5; Graffiti at Blackman Harvey, framed pictures 14/15, 36/7, 38, 39, 46/7, 56/7, 64/5, 68/9, 76/7, 82/3, 92/3, 105, 118, 119; Grayling, upholstered chair 84/5; Habitat, paper blinds 14/15, 36/7, 38, 108/09, 118, 119; C. P. Hart, sanitaryware, taps & showers 118, 119; House of Mirrors, mirrors 64/5, 118; Hypnos Beds, bed 92/3; 14/15, 82/3, 84/5; Lancaster

Carpets, carpet 76/7, 118; Leisure, sink & taps 106, 108/09; John Lewis, ribbons & muslin 56/7, blue felt 76/7, napkins & table mats 105, scales 118; Liberty & Co, fabrics 14/15; Lighting Workshop, wall lights 112/13; London Sofa Bed Centre, sofa beds 36/7, 38, 39, 46/7, 82/3, 84/5; Lower Road Plant Centre, patio plants 82/3; Maison Designs, lamp & glass tables 36/7, metal trolleys 38, 76/7; Marble Hill Fireplaces, fireplace 84/5; Marks & Spencer, plants 46/7, lingerie & jug set 56/7, toiletries, notepaper & towels 76/7, plants 82/3, 84/5, dressing gown & plants 92/3, plants 104/05, 108/09, towels 112/13, plants & mahogany accessories 118, toiletries & jug set 118/19; Marvic Fabrics, window seat fabric 82/3; Mediterranean Ceramics, terracotta urns 68/9, 82/3; Mr Light, brass lamp 14/15, table light 38, wall lights 46/7, bedside light 56/7, uplights 64/5, table lamps 76/7, wall lights 92/3; George Moore & Co, kitchen units 104/05; Muraspec, hessian wall covering 68/9; Neff (UK), oven, hob, washing machine, fridge & extractor hood 104/05, 106/07; Perrings, dining chairs 82/3; Pifco, wok 108/09; Plantation shutters, shutters 92/3; Reject Shop, ceramic pots 14/15, trestle table, chairs & accessories 36/7, 38, 39, cardboard trunks 36/7, cruets, china & cutlery 39, china 46, teacups 56/7, folders 76/7, china 82/3, 84/5, 92/3, 104/05, table & chairs 105, chairs, china & cutlery 106, chairs & china 108/09; Rotaflex Home Lighting Products, recessed downlights 68/9, 82/3, 84/5, 104/05; Sanderson, window seat fabric 14/15, seating fabric, 26, 37, wallpaper fabric 92/3; Shires, sanitaryware 112/13; Silent Gliss shower rail 112/13; Sleepezee, divan bed 76/7; Sony UK waterproof hi fi 118; Sphinx, wall tiles 112/13; Swish Products, curtain poles 14/15, 106; Tarian Design, cushion fabrics 36/7, 38, napkins 39; Toshiba, hi fi equipment 38, TV 76/7; Townsend, fireplace 64/5; Victoria & Edward Antiques Centre, desk & chair 46/7, chairs 68/9, fire irons & chairs 84/5, rocking chair 92/3; Westons of Scandinavia, carpet (Danica S.V.) 92/3; World's End Nurseries, plants & terracotta pots 14/15, 64/5; World's End Tiles, wall tiles 108/09, floor tiles 112/13, tiles 118, 119; F. Wrighton & Sons, kitchen units 106, 108/09.

A special thanks to: Amtico and Leisure for their help on the kitchen featured on pages 106-09; Armstrong for the kitchen on pages 106-09; World's End Tiles for the kitchen on pages 107-09 and the bathroom on pages 112-13.

PHOTOGRAPHIC ACKNOWLEDGEMENTS:
Alno Kitchens UK Ltd 70, 94/95; Amtico/ 'Random Plank' 86/7; B & Q DIY Supercentres 112 above, 117; Barratt Developments/ 'Accord' 112 below; Jon Bouchier/Orbis 20 below, 21 below; Michael Boys 13 below, 32/33, 45 above, 114 below; Richard Bryant/ Arcaid 34/35, 45 below right, 59 left, 60; Camera Press 23 above centre, 69 below, 116 below; Cover Plus Paints/FW Woolworth 88 left; Cover Plus Paints/FW Woolworth (House of Mayfair), Freestyle Collection 6/7; Dulux 1, 35 below, 42 below right, 49 below, 54/55, 59 centre, 116 above; Robert Harding 16/17, (designer: Dawn Marsden) 88/89; Nelson Hargreaves 120; Kingfisher Wallcoverings 50 above left; John Heseltine 23 above right; Maison de Marie Claire/Bouchet/Chauvel 102/ 103;/Bouchet/Puech 61 below;/Chabaneix/ Nahe 50/51;/Chabaneix/Rozensztruch 59 right;/Dirand 114/115;/Duronsoy/Hourdin 24 left, 40/41 below;/Eriaud/Comte/Puech 62/63 below, 100/101;/Hussenot/Belmont 48 above;/ Korniloff/Chauvel 23 below;/Korniloff/Comte 40 above;/Ptaut/Bayle 42 above left, 78/79;/ Ptaut/Bayle/Puech 50 below left;/Ptaut/Puech 42 above right, 90/91;/Real/Belmont 28 left;/ Rozes/Hirsch 86 left, 99 right; Ronseal 71, 91 above and below; Slumberdown 48/49, 74/75; Stag Polka Furniture 34 left; Jessica Strang/ Orbis 20 above; Jessica Strang (Oliver Morgan, architect) 10 above, 17 below, 28 right, 29; (Julia Aldridge, designer) 44 left inset, 44/45; (Lyn Le Grice, designer) 58 above and below; (Lou Klein, designer) 72 above; (Sonny Howson, designer) 97 below; Ron Sutherland 10 below, 17 above; Today Interiors 72/73 below; Elizabeth Whiting and Associates/Jon Bouchier/Isobel Czarska Designs 8/9;/Michael Crockett 49 above;/ David Cripps/Lyn Le Grice 25 right;/Michael Dunne 21 above, 24/25, 66/67, 67 right;/ Michael Dunne/Earl Burn Combs Design 80/ 81;/Michael Dunne/Mary Gilliatt 23 left, 81 below;/Clive Helm 89 right;/Clive Helm/ Gunilla-Stanley 61 above;/Clive Helm/ Campbell Palmer 45 below left;/Ann Kelly 32 below;/Tom Leighton 11 left, 11 right, 12 above, 12 below, 23 centre;/Neil Lorimer 66 left;/Michael Nicholson/Val Arnold 78 left;/ Michael Nicholson/De Wildt 110/111;/Michael Nicholson/John Wright 110 left, 80 left;/Spike Powell 33 below;/Spike Powell/Katherine and James Taylor 98/99;/Tim Street-Porter 111 right, 104 left, 52/53;/Jerry Tubby 13 above;/ Jerry Tubby/Fabian Badcock 98 left; Wrighton International Ltd/'Accent Range' 97 above. All other photography Bruce Hemming All line drawings Stuart Perry